ZOR

Philosophy, Spirituality, and Science

A novel exploring true happiness,

and the importance of positive energy.

By Ray Clements (J.B.)

Copyright © 2012 Ray Clements.
All rights reserved.

ISBN: 1452895406
ISBN-13: 9781452895406
LCCN: 2010907937
CreateSpace, North Charleston, SC

For my two boys, Adam and Tyler;

what Zor can't teach you, you don't need to know.

FORWARD

As a Business School Graduate from the 70's, I have always found it difficult to balance corporate success with peace, love, and understanding. Is it enough to pursue capitalism or are we part of a bigger plan? A voracious student, I have spent decades searching for the answer, finally deciding to write the lesson I could not find.

THE BEGINNING

There are two things you need to know about Zor.

First: the man is brilliant. A native of Haiti, he stands less than five feet tall and boasts broad shoulders and a muscular build. Classically handsome, with mocha skin and European features that suggest mixed ancestry, Zor is charmingly soft-spoken with a disarming Caribbean lilt.

Second: he destroyed my life.

CHAPTER 1

We met one day in late March. It was sunny with temperatures approaching 60 degrees. For most of the country, that may seem cold, but to the residents of Boston, after a long New England winter, 60 degrees is a balmy respite.

Daylight saving time had recently started, so I decided to join the seasonal celebration by taking an early afternoon walk through the Public Garden. Turning a corner by the Duck Pond, I noticed a solitary figure coming off Boylston Street. He was a very short man with a purposeful stride. Something about his gait, gliding more than walking, held my gaze.

As he approached, I realized he wasn't just short, he was a dwarf. I couldn't tell his age, but he walked with a rhythm of confidence.

I was not the only one to notice him. He passed two teenage boys sitting on a park bench. One made a comment that drew laughter from the other. Ignoring them both, the dwarf continued on his way.

Angered by this disregard, the boys jumped to their feet and quickly overtook him. Standing directly in his path, they both started talking; measured at first, it soon became heated. I could not hear what was being said, but the louder the boys spoke, the calmer the dwarf appeared.

Failing to elicit any response, the antagonists became more direct, pointing their fingers and shouting wildly. It was to no avail. The dwarf just stood there, smiling and shaking his head.

No one else seemed to notice what was happening. Fearing for the dwarf's safety, I started towards them to intercede.

The boys quickly tired. Unable to escalate their taunts into an altercation, frustration set in and they stepped aside. The dwarf continued on as the weary tormentors skulked away.

I was stunned. I had to talk to this man and find out how his antagonists had been so easily dispatched. I caught up to him and started a walking conversation.

"Excuse me," I said. "I just saw those two guys harassing you. How did you stay so calm?"

The man smiled and said in a slight Caribbean accent, "I guess it's my nature."

"What were you saying to them each time you shook your head?"

"No, thank you."

"No, thank you?"

"No, thank you."

"What does that mean?"

"I was politely refusing their gift," he said.

"I don't get it."

He stopped walking. "If someone offers you a gift and you refuse to accept it, who then owns the gift?"

"The giver, I guess."

"Exactly. Those boys were trying to give me their gift of negative ch'i."

"Ch'i?"

"Ch'i, life force, karma, their energy. Nothing is more insidious than negative energy. Once accepted, it festers and grows and contaminates your entire being. The only relief is to pass that poison on to someone else. Those boys were filled with negative energy, slowly devouring them like flesh-eating bacteria. They were desperate to unload it onto me, but when they realized I was unwilling to respond in kind, unwilling to share in their anger, unwilling to accept their gift, they had to move on. The weight of their burden was overwhelming."

He fell silent. I wasn't sure what he had just said, but I knew he was done talking.

"Well, anyway, that was quite something to see." I extended my hand. "John. John Brewster."

His hand was small but his grasp firm, much firmer than I expected. He nodded once. "I am Zor." Then he turned and walked away.

CHAPTER 2

Brewster Capital est. 1855

I've walked past that brass placard my entire life. Each time it's been a source of pride. Located at 2 School Street in Boston, Brewster Capital has been managing the assets of the Brewster family for more than 150 years. I am a direct descendant of the founder, William Brewster, and the current asset manager, as was my father before me.

Born in 1778, William Brewster became an accomplished seaman at a very early age. By his twenty-fifth birthday, he was captain of his own ship, and over time parlayed a shrewd profiteering nature into a small fortune.

Family lore holds he made his fortune in molasses. Carrying tobacco and textiles to the West Indies in trade, he would then return with his holds full of molasses. The molasses would be distilled into rum and sold, with the profits being reinvested into larger shipments.

I believed this to be true until my senior year of Academy, where we studied the New England economy of the early 1800s. At the time, the most profitable shipping lanes did not go directly from America to the West Indies; instead, they veered further east to Africa, exchanging rum for slaves, which were then traded for molasses.

I was stunned. It had never occurred to me that Brewster Capital, my family's endowment, was founded on the scarred back of slavery. The next time I was home for a holiday, I put it to my dad. Waiting until after dinner when we were alone in the den, I asked him if Captain Brewster was in fact a slave runner.

If taken by the directness of the question, my dad didn't show it. He paused for a moment, put down the newspaper, and reached for his scotch. "No one knows for sure what the captain did. After all, it was two hundred years ago. I've searched for the answer with little success. I believe, however, educated men like you and me must conclude that William Brewster's great fortune was a result of cargo far more nefarious than molasses." He winked, tapped his nose twice, and went back to his paper.

I miss my dad. He had a way of making me feel special, like we were always sharing an inside joke no one else got. He was the kindest man I ever met. In my entire life, I remember him losing his temper only twice.

The first time happened to be that same weekend I was home. It had nothing to do with Brewster Capital's sordid beginnings; in fact I don't recall ever discussing that again.

What caused my dad's outrage was a surprise visit by his brother Ernest. Eight years younger and a bit of a rake, Ernest had always been trouble. Overweight and pasty-faced with a pencil-thin moustache, he was the antithesis of my dad. He wasn't exactly a black sheep, but his presence usually foretold family chaos. That weekend was no different. Showing up Sunday morning, welcomed but unannounced, he let himself in.

My dad greeted him with a big smile. "Ernest! Come on in. You're just in time to join us for brunch." Nothing was more important to my father than family, regardless of individual character.

Ernest was clutching a copy of Brewster Capital's annual report and brandished it in Dad's face. "Why did you cut the dividend?"

After the death of my grandfather 18 months earlier, the shareholders had overwhelmingly voted to appoint my dad fund manager. Under his stewardship, the net asset value had grown nine percent, more than doubling its average annual return. My father had drastically reduced cash disbursements, believing reinvestment of capital to be a more prudent choice. Ernest had no real job and was living off the fund's dividends.

"I explained it in last year's annual report," my dad said. "We needed to increase the asset growth."

"You can't do that without a vote."

"Blank proxies went out with the statement. Within two weeks I controlled 70% of the voting shares. If you had an objection, you should have called me."

"You knew I was out of the country," Ernest said. "Next to you, I'm the largest shareholder. You should have waited."

"I had no idea where you were or when you would return. I have a fiduciary responsibility to hundreds of shareholders and I can't manage this trust based on your globetrotting schedule."

"Maybe you can't manage this trust at all," my uncle said under his breath.

We were all aware that Ernest had opposed my dad's appointment, questioning his experience and arguing for professional management.

"Please, Ernest." My dad opened his arms toward the dining room. "It's Sunday, let's enjoy our brunch as family, and discuss business tomorrow at School Street."

My uncle shook him off. "This fund has been managed for decades without reducing dividends. Suddenly you take over and the payout is slashed. I knew you couldn't handle this. You could never measure up to Dad and you never will. Let's face it, big brother; you're in over your head."

My dad calmly placed his hand on his brother's shoulder. "If you need cash, I'll buy shares off you at their fair market value. If you want to keep control of your equity, I'll let you margin them. Hell, I'm happy to give you what you need out of my personal funds, no strings attached, but let's transact business tomorrow and enjoy family today."

Ernest headed for the door. "I don't need your charity. I've got options. You might have gotten the proxies this year, but markets correct and shareholders are fickle. This isn't over. Not by a long shot."

Dad excused himself, muttering something about respect, and followed his brother outside. I could not make out what was said, but my father was fuming. I had never seen him like this, punctuating every word with a finger in Ernest's chest. Quickly my uncle's bravado waned, and he soon crawled back into his car and meekly drove away.

When he came back inside, my dad picked up his Bloody Mary and toasted me. "Be thankful you're an only child."

I never liked my uncle. He was arrogant and aloof. Shortly after this encounter, The Who released the rock opera *Tommy*. From then on I took a guilty pleasure in referring to Ernest as Uncle Ernie. I don't think he ever caught on.

The second time I saw my father's ire was a couple months later during Christmas break. I told him of my intention to go to Boston University instead of Harvard.

He was a third-generation legacy student and always assumed I would be a fourth, but in 1969 I considered Harvard's legacy program elitist. I probably would have been accepted on my own merit, but I could never be sure. Besides, BU's diverse student body and its location at Kenmore Square seemed much more interesting than a bunch of rich prep-school kids in Cambridge.

My dad was furious. Shouting so loudly my mother left the room, he raged that the only tuition bill he was paying was to The Crimson, and if I chose to go somewhere else, it would be my cost to bear.

I made it clear the only school I was attending was BU. Further, if he was refusing to fund my education, then he might as well drive me to a recruiting office because without a student deferment I would be in Nam by July 4th. This may have been a cheap threat, but I had known for some time that my dad was the only person more concerned with my draft status than me.

Eventually he came around. The Vietnam War forced the issue. I've often wondered if BU was the better choice. I enjoyed college immensely, but an Ivy League degree would have provided a certain gravitas for my professional life. There is one thing I still have from Boston University, however, that I could never have gotten at Harvard: my wife, Mary.

I met her my senior year. She was a sophomore transfer from Regis College. Separated by just 20 miles, the two schools were at opposite ends of the educational spectrum. Regis, supported by the Roman Catholic Church, was an all-women's school founded on the principles of virtue and piety. Boston University at the time was a bastion of sex, drugs, and rock 'n' roll.

Mary matriculated well.

The first weekend at school found us both at the same mixer. Somehow I convinced her to come back to my place. She wouldn't sleep with me that night, but there was enough slap-and-tickle to keep me interested. I took her out the next weekend, and we've been together ever since.

Senior year at Boston University was the best of all. With most of my requirements for a business degree already met, I was able to pursue my true interest, the social sciences. Influenced by professors like Murray Levin, Howard Zinn, and Eli Weisel, those were heady times. While in college I saw the drinking age reduced, the draft abolished, a corrupt president resign, and marijuana practically decriminalized. For the first time in my life, the government really seemed to be for the people, by the people.

We were out of Nam, and the conflict was nearing its end. Though ecstatic with this outcome, it left many my age confused. The war had been the central theme of our lives since high school. We read about it, discussed it, debated it, and feared it. We dedicated our lives to its abolition. With the conflict waning, we were losing our focus.

The music, the drugs, the war's end, everything pointed to a new society, one crafted and nurtured by our generation, a society that would be more powerful at peace than it ever could be at war. This is what I wanted to be a part of, but I didn't know how.

Then one night, while getting stoned in the Combat Zone, it came to me. Actually, it came to my roommate, Ed.

CHAPTER 3

It was a Thursday night in the spring of '74 and Ed had joined me to score some pot. Friends since freshman orientation, Ed and I were tight. We had both scheduled our classes for Tuesday, Wednesday, and Thursday, assuring a four-day weekend throughout the year. Thursday night was always boys' night out, and every other week we had to feed Kong.

Kong had been with us since the beginning. The first Saturday on campus, Ed and I went downtown to a head shop. We were just going to buy some rolling papers, but Ed was immediately drawn to Kong, a twelve-inch ceramic gorilla. Seated on a throne, with the bowl at his navel and a hole in his head, Kong was King.

Ed laid down the 12 bucks. "It's not just a bong, it's a statement."

When we got back to the dorm, we built Kong an appropriate shrine, and he maintained a place of prominence from that day on.

Buying pot on campus senior year had become complicated because availability was too erratic. We needed a source we could count on and searched throughout the city. Eventually we discovered Jake's, a hotel and bar nestled between Boston's Combat Zone and the Theater District.

Jake's had cheap rooms, cheap booze, and a full late-night menu, but back in the '70s you went there for two things: ass or grass. We were never interested in the hookers, just the pot.

The Thursday-night routine was always the same: Frye boots, straight-leg jeans, concert T-shirt and denim jackets. Jake's was in a tough section of town, and to keep from being hassled, you didn't have to be tough, but you had to look it.

We'd take the Green Line to Boylston Street and walk the final two blocks, arriving around 8:30. It was early, but Jake's always had a groove. The location assured an eclectic group of strippers, transvestites, entertainers, and drifters just off the Greyhound bus.

Filled with old queens and young hustlers (Ed often remarked that Jake's was one midget shy of a Fellini movie), you never knew what to expect. Regardless of the crowd, there were always empty seats at the bar. If you wanted to drink, you sat at a table or stood. If you wanted to do business, you sat at the bar, and when the business was done, so were you.

ZOR

Like every other Thursday, Ed and I sat down and ordered two beers at a dollar each. I took a long pull, put down three singles to cover the bill and tip, then caught the bartender's eye and added two twenties. As we drank our beers, he picked up the money and whispered something to a waiter, who went into the men's room. A moment later, he came back out and gave me a slight nod.

I got up, went in, and found a couple of one-ounce bags of pot secured above the urinal. Not the classiest exchange, but it served its purpose. What I liked most about Jake's was their policy of adding a loose joint to every bag so you could enjoy the product on the way home. To top it off, the pot was free. We would keep one ounce for ourselves and sell the other at school for $40. We had pot all year long, and it never cost us a nickel.

We left our beer unfinished and went outside to share a joint. While smoking in the alley next to Jake's, Ed suggested we check out the strippers at the Two O'clock Lounge.

I rarely went to strip joints. Mary didn't like the idea, and besides, I was getting all I could handle at home, but Ed insisted. We sat down at the bar and ordered two Buds, careful to turn the labels towards the bartender so that he couldn't tell when the beer was gone and pressure us into another. At $8 a pop we were drinking slowly.

ZOR

Within minutes, a couple of pros were on each side of us, rubbing our backs and asking to join us for a drink. We were high, not stupid. They were attractive enough, but their Adam's apples were bigger than ours. Politely declining, Ed and I left the bar. We crossed Tremont Street and went into the Public Garden to spark up our second joint. It was there Ed planned our future.

"Nixon's done," he said.

"From your lips to God's ears." I took another hit.

"No, I mean it. Nixon's done. Tomorrow, the day after, or the day after that. It's just a matter of time before Ford is sworn in." We both started laughing at the absurdity of Gerald Ford being our next president. There was a long pause before he continued. "Nixon's gone and the war is over. What are we going to do?"

"Dance in the streets, I guess."

He wasn't amused. "For the past six years my life had meaning. I had a purpose. Nam and Nixon, Nixon and Nam, all I thought about was saving the world from both of them. Everything else was secondary. Now, what's the point?"

"There'll be other causes."

"Where? We've won. The conservative movement and all it stands for is dead, the Pentagon Papers saw to that. There won't be another war in our lifetime and racism's a thing of the past. The women's movement, gay rights, recreational drug use, it's all cool. There's nothing left to fight for."

"Give me five for that, my man."

Our joint was done. Fortunately, I had a backup behind my right ear. I pulled it out, lit it and hit it. "Maybe we should hike across Europe. Throw some stuff in a knapsack and get lost for a year."

Ed studied me for some time. "I said I didn't know what *I* was going to do after graduation. I know what *you're* going to do. You're a trust-fund kid. You're going to live on Wall Street." He leaned in close and sniffed twice. "I can smell money all over you."

I laughed. When you're high, everything seems funny. Later it occurred to me Ed wasn't joking.

"I'm thinking of South America," he said. "Poverty, oppression, tyranny... Maybe I can make a difference down there."

Now it was my turn to lean in at him. "Are you insane? We barely dodged Nam and now you want to volunteer for another war in another country?"

"Not a war, a coup. Besides, I'm not talking about military service, I'm talking about public disobedience, you know, organized dissent."

"Preaching dissent in a banana republic will get you killed, jailed, or climbing the mountains with a M-16.

If we're going to save the world, we should do it as angels of peace, not war."

Our last joint was gone. Ed started eating the roach as we walked back to Boylston station. "Maybe we should just join the Peace Corps."

Again, we both laughed.

This last remark took a couple of seconds to register, but when it did, I stopped dead in my tracks. "Why not?"

"Why not what?"

"Why not join the Peace Corps?" I said. "We could go to Africa."

Ed thought for a moment then smiled. "It could work."

"What do you mean, could? It's brilliant! We join the Peace Corps, go to Africa, dig some wells, plant some corn, and save a village. No fighting, no guns, no worries." I was ecstatic. Not only would this keep my best friend out of the Nicaraguan mountains, it would provide me some much-needed adventure.

I had been worried about my post graduate options for some time. I loved my dad, but I didn't love his life. A career of sitting at a desk and reading the *Wall Street Journal* seemed like early death. Now I had something to look forward to.

Suddenly I had a troubling thought. "What if we go all the way to Africa only to discover we're no good as ambassadors of peace?

"Better to fail at something you love than succeed at something you hate."

We traveled back to the dorm in agreement, silently enjoying our buzz.

CHAPTER 4

Mary took the news well. I knew she would. We were deeply in love, inseparable even, but the Peace Corps was months away. We still had the rest of the school year, and she chose to live in the moment, which is what I liked most about her.

My dad was a different story. He had been anticipating my ascension to Brewster Capital since I was in prep school. Choosing Boston University over Harvard was tough enough for him to accept (though he eventually chalked it up to the times and "revolution in the air"). I couldn't imagine his reaction to my choice of Africa over School Street.

One day over drinks I casually told him. He didn't seem to hear me, so I said it again. "Dad, I'm going to Africa with the Peace Corps after graduation."

"I heard you the first time." I had never before seen him at a loss for words. "When do you leave?"

"End of the summer, I think. We'll need time to get our shots and pull the paperwork together."

"We?"

"Ed and me."

His face tightened. He never liked Ed, blaming his middle-class activism for my radical tendencies. "You guys still chasing dreams, trying to save the world?"

"What's wrong with that? When you stop chasing dreams all that's left are nightmares."

"When I was a child I spake as a child, I understood as a child, I thought as a child; but when I became a man, I put away childish things." I just smiled; he would never understand. He closed one eye and tapped his nose twice. "You know, when you decide to swim with the current instead of against it, life becomes pretty easy."

"It's more than swimming against the current, Dad. It's living with a purpose. It's recognizing that we're all in this together and accepting that responsibility."

My dad smiled and repeated one of his favorite quotes. "A young conservative may have no heart, but an old liberal has no brains."

"Dad, I need to do this, with or without your support."

After a moment he touched his glass to mine and looked me in the eye. "No worries then."

I should have known better.

The remainder of my senior year proceeded swimmingly. I graduated with honors, having maintained Dean's List for eight consecutive semesters. My folks sent Mary and me to Bermuda as a graduation present. They paid for everything, all first class.

In retrospect, I think it was the first time Mary got a taste of how good our lifestyle could be. When we got back home, my dad pulled another surprise. He had rented a summer sublet for me on Beacon Hill. It was small with two bedrooms but perfect for a young couple playing house.

Before I had a chance to ask, Mary moved in. She told her parents she was staying in Boston to take some extra classes, but all we studied that summer was the *Kama Sutra*. Neither of us worked. I had received almost $2,000 in graduation gifts and we lived off that.

Walks along the Charles, picnics in the Common, cocktails at sunset on our deck—there is nothing more romantic than summer in Boston.

Ed and I also kept in contact throughout the summer. By mid-August we had all the documents processed and the inoculations we needed.

The evening my dad called was exactly two weeks before we were to leave. He wanted to take Mary and me to lunch one more time and suggested Locke-Ober at noon. Mary wasn't feeling well that day so I went alone.

I got there five minutes late and saw my dad drain his first martini. As I sat down he ordered us both another and the Finnan Haddie. His angst was obvious.

"What's wrong?" I asked.

"Ernest. He's taking over Brewster Capital."

"What?"

"He came by the office this morning and informed me of his intention to stage a proxy fight next month at the annual meeting. Nothing personal, he said. He just thinks we could all benefit from some new blood."

"His blood is eighty proof!"

"He doesn't want to manage it directly. He wants to bring in professionals. Since graduating from Princeton two years ago, your cousin has been climbing the ranks at Merrill Lynch. Ernest thinks we should give the fund to their trust management division."

"Who cares what he thinks? You control seventy percent of the stock."

"I did once, but who knows? I haven't needed to confirm those voting rights for years. He wouldn't be giving notice of a fight if he didn't think he had the votes needed."

We finished our drinks and got two more.

"What are you going to do?"

He smiled. "Maybe I'll move to Boca and retire."

"Dad, you're the fund and the fund is you. It's the reason you get out of bed each day. If you want to retire, fine, but retire on your terms, not Uncle Ernie's."

He stared down into his drink. "Maybe he's right. When I started working with your grandfather, we traded off the ticker. Many days, we had nothing to do. Now the markets are so volatile I barely have time to breath. It's become more than a one-man job."

"What's your performance been like?" I tried to sound upbeat.

"Growth is better than average, but cash distribution is low. Ernest has everyone convinced better management will mean both growth and income."

Lunch arrived, but we were no longer hungry. My dad asked the waiter to put everything on his tab. With little more to say, we finished our drinks and left. Before separating, he gave me a hug, told me he loved me, and made me promise to stop by at least one more time before leaving.

I went straight home. Mary was feeling better, and I relayed the day's events. We talked for a long time.

"Maybe your dad will like retirement."

"My dad is at the top of his game. It would kill him."

"If the majority of the shareholders want professional management, they should have professional management."

"My dad is a professional manager." I was taken aback by her lack of concern.

Mary reached over and held my hand. "Honey, I know you love your dad, I love him too, but this is not your problem. It's his." Her cold-hearted assessment again caught me by surprise. "We have less than two weeks together. Let's make the most of it."

I pulled my hand away. "He needs me."

"What are you going to do?"

"The same thing he would do for me."

"What's that?"

"Whatever it takes." I headed out the door.

It was 4 p.m. If I hurried I could still catch him at the office. I wasn't sure what I was going to do, but I was sure I was going to do something.

When I walked in I was shocked to see Uncle Ernie standing there. My dad was getting off the phone. They both seemed surprised to see me.

"What's he doing here?" I asked.

"Be civil, son," Dad said. "We're still family."

I gathered myself together and walked up to my uncle. "My dad has dedicated his life to the management of Brewster Capital. You and your son will never take it over as long as we breathe."

"Over four hundred shareholders depend on this fund," my uncle said. "New financial instruments come to the market every day. It's too much responsibility for one man, even your dad realizes he can't keep up."

I looked over at my dad, but he was staring at the floor. Suddenly I heard myself speak. "My dad and I addressed this earlier today."

They both seemed surprised by this statement, as was I, but there was no turning back now.

ZOR

"He offered me a position." I looked over at my dad. "An *interim* position and I accepted. I'll specifically be researching new investment opportunities throughout the financial markets. He'll still have full management responsibility but I'll act as his research assistant. Once things are in order, we'll petition the shareholders to make the position permanent and secure my replacement."

I stepped closer to Ernie, looking him in the eye. "Your proxy fight is dead. You may think you have the votes now, but I intend to notify every shareholder of this new development. I'll also remind them of the superlative stewardship my father has provided to their financial well-being. My dad may be too humble to sing his own praise, but I'm not, and when I'm done, both my father's position as trust manager and your position as family sot will be secured."

My uncle's face turned beet red, but before he could speak, my dad ushered me out of the office and asked me to wait in the lobby while he had a private moment with his brother.

A few minutes later, Ernie came out of the office and walked past me without a word. I went in to find my dad pouring us a celebratory scotch.

"Brilliant!" He handed me a glass. "I've never been so proud. I knew you'd do the right thing. I knew it."

"It's a short-term solution, Dad. I'm here until we can find you a permanent assistant. I figure that'll take four, five, maybe six months, then I'm gone. Six months, Dad, tops. In six months I'm off to Africa."

"Yes, yes, of course. Six months is all I'll need. So much can happen in six months."

We toasted our success and drained our glasses.

"Let's get started then," I said. "Where's the directory of shareholders?"

"In the cabinet. Why?"

"We better start calling them and let them know my decision. You can bet Uncle Ernie's already formulating a new plan."

"No need." My dad took the phone from my hand. "Ernest backed off. With you staying on, he knows he can't get the votes. We've won."

It seemed too easy, but my dad was adamant. We spoke for another 20 minutes and agreed my first day would be the Monday after Labor Day. Before I left, he called the Ritz and made a dinner reservation for two, telling me to take Mary out and celebrate, on his tab.

Later, while Mary was getting ready, I poured myself a drink and made the call. Ed was at home with his folks in Yonkers for the summer.

"Hey, man, it's me."

He didn't miss a beat. "I've been expecting this call. Who made you back out, your dad or your wife?"

There was a long pause.

"It's not like that. It's a personal issue and I've got to take care of it."

More silence.

"I'm not backing out," I said. "Just a delay, two, three, six months at the most. I'll be there by February."

"February."

"I was thinking, why don't you do the same? Take some time. Enjoy New York. Spend Christmas with your family. Then we both go over the beginning of next year and kick ass."

"What do I do when you cancel again?"

"I'm not cancelling!"

"John, I've been here all summer, I'm sick of New York, my family doesn't celebrate Christmas, we're Jewish, remember? The plane leaves in two weeks and I'm going to be on it."

"All right, relax. Go out now, learn the ropes, and get the lay of the land. I'll be there before you finish digging the first well."

"Sure, man."

"Look, I'm coming."

"Whatever you say, I've got to go. Thanks for the call." He hung up without saying goodbye.

I never spoke with Ed again.

CHAPTER 5

The evening may have started badly, but by our second bottle of Dom Perignon, the mood lightened. You can't be sad at the Ritz. The food was superb, the atmosphere elegant, and Mary beautiful. We discussed our future over the Cocoa Grand Marnier soufflé.

Mary still had to go back to school in the fall, so I rented a luxury apartment on Babcock Street across from West Campus. She had a dorm room in name only, living with me from the outset.

Life at Babcock Towers was idyllic. Not only was I making more money than any of our friends, I was actually enjoying my job. Researching financial markets was fascinating, and I developed a real mathematical flair.

Working with my dad reintroduced me to the finer things in life. Though still in college, Mary showed a maturity beyond her years, holding her own when entertaining or being entertained. We both revelled at being part of Boston's social scene.

I developed a fast friendship with a dozen other financial professionals. We dubbed ourselves the Brahmin Boys and met each Friday in a private room at Locke's. Needless to say, there was little talk of Africa come February.

I would like to say I enjoyed helping the shareholders and felt a real sense of accomplishment, but that would be a lie. The truth is, my dad was extremely generous and I was seduced by the money.

I believe the Peace Corps tried to contact me twice. I never returned their calls. Springtime in Boston found me solidly a part of Brewster Capital and enjoying every minute of it. Mary's birthday was in April, and I surprised her with a diamond. Engaged for over a year, we had a June wedding in the summer of '76.

It was a couple weeks before the bicentennial, and our honeymoon continued through the country's celebration. The night before my wedding, I asked my dad what his secret was to maintaining a successful marriage.

He thought for a moment, tapped his nose twice and winked. "If your wife never sees you totally sober, she won't be able to tell when you've been drinking."

CHAPTER 6

After marriage our lives followed a natural progression. We had two sons, Adam and Tyler, bought a house, and took some vacations. Through all the ups and downs, I remained at Brewster Capital. When my dad passed away a couple years ago, I became the trust's sole manager.

Urban renewal caused every city to gentrify, and Boston was no different. San Francisco lost the Tenderloin, New York lost Times Square, and Boston lost the Combat Zone. The strip clubs and porn shops may have been banished to suburbia, but Jake's persevered. I believe the same family has owned the bar for half a century.

I've often thought Jake's was the classic barometer of Boston's social scene. In the late '70s it stopped catering to seedy transients. Management installed a sound system, dance floor and disco ball. A few years later, the bar went cowboy with a mechanical bull and live country music.

That fad was over before it began, and soon Jake's was filled with overstuffed chairs and plants. The disco music came back along with topless male servers in leather pants, and Jake's became the most notorious gay club in New England.

It was a wild four years, but public protests by the conservative right caused the owners to rethink their business plan and eventually decide to lease the property to a national chain. That was the bar's darkest hour. For three long years patrons dealt with perky waitresses, birthday songs, and red vests covered with silly pieces of flair.

It was a five-year lease but thankfully, because of the lack of business, corporate paid the penalty and broke it after three. Jake's then went from grunge bar to tiki bar (complete with grass skirts and coconut bras), to cigar bar, to martini bar to what it is now; an upscale bar for transients.

Through its many transformations, four things remained constant: the red neon sign over the door, the oak bar along the back wall, the full-length mirror behind the bar, and me.

Early in my professional career I adopted Jake's as my personal sanctuary. I left work every day at 4:30 and headed over to Jake's for two hours of therapy. I never brought my dad, my wife, or any of the Brahmin Boys. I went to Jake's to be alone.

My dad always went to Locke-Ober after work. There he would meet up with old friends he had known for decades. They would drink, talk, laugh, and reminisce. He never understood my affinity for Jake's. I couldn't put it into words, but every time I walked through those doors, just for a moment, I was taken to simpler days, days of Levi's, dollar drafts, and Kong.

One day—actually it was Good Friday—I walked in and sat down as the bartender set up my scotch. Many people want to go to a bar where they know your name; I just want to go where they know my drink.

The financial markets were closed, but I'd still spent my day at the office. The boys would be home from college for Easter, and I didn't want any work over the weekend.

I missed my boys. When they were young we hid baskets full of candy each year. Waking at dawn, they would run through house with squeals of laughter, overlooking the most obvious locations. Mary always provided hints, assuring eventual success.

I remembered the smell of baby powder, their small hands in mine, and the joy only young fatherhood brings. I looked in the mirror behind the bar, smiling at an old man where a young man once sat. Trying to cheer up, I recalled my dad's favorite toast. "Growing old may be hard, but it's better than the alternative."

It was a slow Friday, and I sat at the bar in silence. A middle-aged woman in a faded orange pantsuit sat a few stools down and ordered a draft, "something brewed in Boston" she drawled nasally. It was obvious she was a tourist looking for local flavor. We shared a smile. Unfortunately she read more into it than I intended, and she started to talk.

"How ya doin'?"

"Fine." I turned back to my drink.

Her beer arrived, and she moved to the seat next to me and extended her hand. "I'm Beth."

"Hello, Beth, I'm John."

"John! That's a Boston name, for sure."

I just smiled.

"Don't worry, John, I see your ring. You're married. I'm married too." She gave a big smile and held out her left hand. "I'm meeting my husband here. We split up for the day. I went shopping; he took a tour of Fenway Park. Have you ever been to Fenway Park?"

"Once or twice." I motioned the bartender for another drink.

"You work around here?" she asked.

I nodded.

"What do you do?"

"Money manager."

Beth's eyes grew wide as she could barely contain her excitement. "Oh, my God! That's what my Harry does. He sells insurance. He's been doing it now for fifteen months. He won us this trip to Boston. He was the office rookie of the year, beating out five other salesmen. How long have you been selling insurance?"

My head was about to explode. I should have congratulated her and just shut up, but the scotch was working, and she was annoying.

"I don't sell insurance, I manage assets. I have over five hundred people who depend on me for their financial well-being. I trade in stocks, bonds, commodities and all their derivatives. Every trade I make is a matter of public record and open to scrutiny. I have outperformed the market fifteen years running, and people still complain."

I took a deep breath and continued. "I buy low and sell high, but if I don't buy at the exact low and sell at the exact high, someone bitches. Furthermore, on the rare occasion when I do buy and sell at the perfect levels, someone complains that I didn't invest enough. I am audited quarterly by the city, the state, and the federal government. I field calls all day long, either from shareholders who want me to research some inane investment idea some friend told them about, or from vendors like your husband who want to sell me insurance."

I closed my eyes and composed my exit line. "Having said all this, I'm not whining. This is the life I built, and I'm happy with it. I just wanted you to know I don't sell insurance."

I hoped I hadn't been too rough on her. Evidently I underestimated her Midwestern resolve. She was still smiling.

"Don't be such a gloomy Gus. It takes twice as many muscles to frown as it does to smile."

"I wasn't frowning."

"No, but you sound a little depressed. Maybe you have a chemical imbalance. My Harry takes a pill for that. You should try it. It's made all the difference in the world."

Depressed. Of course I was depressed, but not *chemically* depressed. I was *intellectually* depressed. Having reached a stage in life where everything should be easier, things had become more difficult. No, not difficult, complicated. Rather than share that all with Beth, I decided to take a more neutral approach.

"I'm not saying my life is bad, I'm just saying how my life is. I don't make value judgments. We all deserve the life we live. My life is a direct result of the choices I've made, but in retrospect I realize some of those choices may have been wrong. It has nothing to do with clinical depression. Remorse is simply a by-product of self-evaluation. We all have regrets. It's totally natural. You can't be happy all the time."

My mouth was on a roll again, and I tagged along for the ride. I turned to her. "My problem is not that I'm depressed, but that depression has become a mental disorder.

Depression is not a crisis; it's a natural state of being. You used to be able to have regrets without worrying about being analyzed. I don't need a doctor and I don't need a pill, what I need is solitude."

"There's Harry now! Nice talking to ya." She laid ten dollars on the bar and tottered off.

I returned to my drink, thankful she never said "You betcha."

I was getting ready to pay the tab when I heard a voice say, "Deal, don't dwell." I say I heard it but that's not completely true, it was more like I felt it. The words were not just coming to me, they were coming *through* me.

I looked around but saw no one at the bar. Then I looked in the mirror and saw his reflection. Surprisingly, he was sitting right next to me. It had been weeks since I met him in the Public Garden, but the encounter had stayed fresh in my mind.

It was Zor.

CHAPTER 7

"Hey, it's great to see you again." I slapped him on the back and realized he was much more solid than he looked. He returned my smile.

"Jake," I called, "Jake, come over here." (Over the years, all the bartenders have been called Jake.) He arrived and laid down a coaster. "Jake, I want you to meet someone. This is the guy I was telling you about, the guy who was hassled in the Public Garden a couple weeks ago." He didn't seem to make the connection. "Zor, this is Zor."

"Oh, yeah, good to meet you, Thor, what can I get you?"

"Thor is the Norse god of thunder. My name is Zor."

"Zor?"

"Zor."

"Alright then, Zor, what'll you have?"

"Makers Mark, neat."

When the drink arrived, Zor tipped his glass in my direction before taking a sip.

"You work around here?" I asked.

"No."

"Live in the area?"

"Not really."

"Well, what brings you here?"

He smiled. "Makers Mark, neat."

After a moment's silence, he asked in a much more serious tone, "What brings you here?"

I raised my drink to the broken clock, stuck at 5:10. "If it's five o'clock, I'm here."

"Every day? Rain or shine, good or bad, winter, spring, summer and fall?"

"This is my time." I tried not to sound defensive. "My time to unwind."

"Unwind or avoid?"

I turned to pay my bar tab. "What did you mean?"

"When?"

"Deal, don't dwell."

He raised his eyebrows. "You heard that?"

"You're sitting right next to me, of course I heard it. What did you mean?"

"I meant deal, don't dwell."

I sighed and waited.

"Deal with your problems, don't dwell on them. Concentrating on life's negatives debilitates the soul. Identify the cause of this negative energy and rid it from your life."

I half smiled. "If I rid my life of everything that depresses me, I'd have a very empty life."

"On the contrary, it would finally be full."

"My life is full. In fact my life is pretty damn good. No complaints."

"You seemed to be complaining a minute ago."

"That was just drunk talk."

"You're drunk?"

"They call it work for a reason," I said. "If it were fun, they'd call it vacation. Besides, my job is the best part of the day."

"Is that why you're here?" He eyed my wedding band. "To keep from going home to your wife?"

"To unwind from my job. I love going home to my wife."

Zor smiled. "Methinks he doth protest too much."

I forgot about paying my tab and ordered another drink. When it arrived, I continued talking, more to myself than anyone else. "I'm not saying things are perfect. I met my wife in college, perhaps the bloom is a bit off the rose. We've been married over thirty years. Our love has matured."

"How so?"

For a moment I thought back to our days at Boston University. "That mind-numbing, pulse-racing, all-encompassing infatuation matures into a more rational long-lasting marriage. One that can deal with children and commitments and stress. It's healthy for passion to evolve into compassion."

"Maybe, but it sounds boring to me."

"Boring?" I laughed. "Believe me, there's nothing boring about my marriage."

Zor leaned in, and for some reason I did the same. "Do you love your wife?" he asked.

"Of course. And she loves me. I'm just not sure if she likes me all that much. Passion gets replaced with a comfortable interdependence. It's like Springsteen says, 'All them things that seemed so important, vanished right into air; I act like I don't remember, Mary acts like she don't care.'"

"You seem to have lost your connection."

I slapped the top of the bar. "Exactly! That's the term I was looking for, *connection, connection, connection.* There was a time when we were totally connected. She was the yin to my yang. Now we coexist."

We both fell silent for a couple minutes.

"What would you say if I could give her back to you?" he said.

His tone was chilling and his comment caught me off-guard. What had I gotten myself into?

"I don't mean give her back in body but in spirit. What would you say if I could return your relationship, your marriage, back to those mind-numbing days?"

I stayed silent.

"Don't worry," he said. "This is no Faustian bargain, I ask for nothing in return."

More to myself than anyone else, I said, "I would give anything to have us back to the way we were."

"It's really quite simple. You just need to recognize cause and effect. Everything is the result of something else. To have what you have not, you must do what you do not."

CHAPTER 8

We spoke for another thirty minutes, neither of us touching our drinks (even I know there's a limit when I'm driving).

"The problem with your marriage," Zor said, "has nothing to do with your actual relationship. The problem is rooted in your neuron networks."

"Our what?"

"Your brains or, more accurately, the way you two are allowing your brains to process your emotions."

"You lost me."

Zor explained the concept of associative memory and neural networks. The brain is made up of tiny nerve cells called neurons. Each neuron has branches that connect to other neurons creating the neuron network. This three-dimensional web exists throughout the brain and determines our actions, feelings, and thoughts.

Every idea or experience we have is captured on a neuron branch. We immediately associate the event with whatever emotions we are feeling at the time, which causes additional neuron branches to attach, thus creating a web of thought. Initially, the connection is weak, but every time we recall that experience, bonded with the emotion, we strengthen the association.

"For example," he said, "where did you meet your wife?"

"At a college party."

"A party, where you're attractive, charming, and funny. These perceptions generate pleasant emotions. This is the beginning of her John Brewster neuron network. This is why first impressions are so critical. Every time she thinks of you, 'attractive, charming and funny' are reinforced. Eventually these pleasant thoughts cause an emotional high that puts you at the center of the evening. Everything that happens at the party is now part of the John Brewster experience. All of her emotions and feelings will be associated with you through her neural web.

"Furthermore, the web expands every time you interact. As you date, go to parties, concerts, romantic dinners, she now associates these positive experiences with you. Even though her enjoyment of a Bruce Springsteen concert may have had nothing to do with your presence, the positive feeling the concert generated will still be part of the neuron net she attributes to you. Eventually all of these emotions continue to reinforce each other and develop into love. The question is, does she love John Brewster or the John Brewster experience?"

"Are you saying my wife doesn't love me?"

"I'm saying many people become lovers long before they become friends, and if that love is based on the experience rather than the person, it has little chance to endure."

"I'm the same person I was in college. If she loved me then, she should love me now."

"You're not even the same person you were yesterday, but that's not the point. Neuron connections are strengthened by repeated use. If we stop reinforcing these connections, they eventually dissolve and new ones are created. If your wife's feelings have changed, it's because her neuron network that interprets the John Brewster experience has changed."

"How can I be responsible for her interpretations? We've been together since the early seventies, it can't all be fun and games. I've been a loving husband, given her two great kids, and a lifestyle most women would kill for."

"You're missing the point. No one is responsible for their interpretations, at least not consciously. We're hopelessly addicted to our emotional needs. These needs are filled by the neuron network. Subconsciously, we pursue the ideas that create positive emotions and avoid the ideas that produce negative emotions. It doesn't matter what we want on a conscious level. If your wife's neuron net is wired to interpret the John Brewster experience negatively, there's nothing she can do. Her emotional desires will rule the day."

"If it's hopeless, why are we talking about it?"

"Fighting our emotional addictions is hopeless. Restructuring our neuron networks is not. Many people have successfully cured addictions, but to do so you must fight at the subconscious level where the addiction manifests."

"Maybe that works for addicts, but—"

"We're all addicted to our emotional needs. Don't get caught up in the terminology." Zor paused to ask Jake for a glass of water. "You may be surprised to learn that your wife is as unhappy as you are with the marriage."

"If she were unhappy, she could change things."

"You're not listening. Even if she wanted to change, she wouldn't be able to. Addictions are insidious. We all know people addicted to bad behaviors. They may want to quit their addictions in the worst way, but they can't. It takes more than recognition to end an addiction, it takes restructuring. You and your wife have lost your positive emotional connections."

I reluctantly nodded.

"All you need to do is cognitively restructure your thought process."

My head stopped mid-nod.

"That may sound complicated, but it's really quite simple. You must start associating positive emotional feelings with each other. Since you no longer do this on a subconscious level, you and your wife must make a cognitive effort. Neurons that fire together wire together. As these emotional associations strengthen, they'll become grounded in your subconscious, affecting your feelings with no awareness or control. The two of you will be like lovestruck teenagers again."

"Sounds like something out of *The Manchurian Candidate*." For the second time that evening, I began looking for an exit line.

"There's nothing sinister about this technique. It's used every day by hypnotists who put a subject's objective mind to sleep in order to communicate directly with the subconscious and create a new neuron connection, one that associates a negative emotion with the addiction. The patient has no idea what happened but, if it's done right, suddenly stops craving tobacco."

"So I'm going to save my marriage by hypnotizing my wife?"

"Hypnotic suggestion would certainly work, but I'm afraid any results would be short-lived. We need a more permanent solution to your problem. Tell me what happens when you go home at night."

"Nothing unusual, we have a big house and most of the evening we try not to get in each other's way."

"How romantic."

"I get in around seven-thirty and check the mail as Mary finishes making dinner. I'll open a bottle of wine and bring it to the table. Over the meal we discuss our day, and then I clean up while she goes upstairs. She's usually in bed by nine and I join her after the eleven-o'clock news."

"Not exactly a Harlequin romance."

"Our relationship has matured."

"And you're no longer connected."

"It seems we're just going through the motions of marriage. It wasn't so obvious when the boys were around, they brought us all together as a family. But unless they're home from college, Mary goes her way and I go mine."

"What do you mean, 'discuss your day'?"

"Whatever happened—challenges we met, the problems we solved, stuff like that."

Zor smiled. "Every night?"

"Like clockwork."

"There's the problem! You're reinforcing each other's negative ch'i."

Again with the Ch'i? This guy's obsessed.

"Each evening when you and your wife discuss the problems of the day, you revisit the negative energy. In fact you increase its destructive power by transferring it back and forth. This negative energy creates disharmony. To change your relationship you must change your evening routine."

"Scotch instead of wine?"

"Very funny. When Mary asks you about your day, share only the positives."

"What if nothing positive happened?"

"If you go through an entire day without noticing something positive, it says a lot more about you than it does about your day."

"Okay, okay, tonight I'll try happy talk."

"This isn't about patronizing your wife. It's about creating a flow of positive emotional energy. You can't simply ask her how her day went; ask her to tell you something good. And not just tonight, every night. Make it a point to exchange positive energy, and only positive energy. This will re-establish a level of positive emotional associations that will pave the way back for some of the passion your marriage has lost.

"All right," I said. "I'll try it."

"Don't try it, do it."

"All right, I'll do it."

Zor wasn't done. "Next, you must re-establish the bedroom."

"I like the sound of that."

"This has nothing to do with sex."

"My wife will like the sound of that."

He shot me a look. "There is no more vulnerable time for couples than when they go to bed. You both have exploited this negatively."

"Who told you that?"

"You did, you told me you no longer go to bed at the same time. Forget about sex, you two are afraid to be together. Remember in the beginning, the connection you two had in bed? It was physical, but more than that, it was intimate. You chose that time not just to have sex, but to communicate. That communication has been lost. Now your wife's afraid to talk to you for fear you'll interpret her overtures sexually, and you're afraid to talk to her for fear she won't. Rather than deal with this negative energy, you both choose avoidance. It's a common remedy but deadly to a relationship."

He was starting to make sense.

"Tonight, go to bed when your wife does and start a new tradition. Before falling asleep, you should exchange one trait you sincerely appreciate about each other. No repeats. Each night you must come up with something new. At first your wife will be suspicious."

"This sounds like a segment of Dr. Phil."

"Don't mock what you don't understand. She'll assume you're fishing for sex. You can't blame her. When was the last time you went to bed with her and didn't try?"

I shrugged and looked away.

He reached for the bar bill. "And lastly, in the morning when you leave for work, regardless of what awaits, tell your wife you expect to have a great day and will fill her in on the details when you get home."

"She's not an idiot; she's bound to see through all this."

"So?"

"You expect such an obvious ploy to actually save my marriage."

He hopped off his barstool. "I expect it will save your life."

CHAPTER 9

My house in Brookline is less than thirty minutes out of Boston. I pulled onto our street and saw empty trash barrels and recycle bins in every driveway. My grip on the steering wheel tightened—it was Friday and I had forgotten to put out the trash even though my wife had made a point of reminding me the night before. I knew she would be less than thrilled.

She was standing at the doorway as I walked in.

"I know," I said. "Sorry."

"I asked you to do one thing, and you couldn't be bothered. I had to run out as the trash men were driving up the street. I hadn't showered, I wasn't dressed. Thanks." She turned back towards the living room.

"I said I'm sorry. I hate recycling anyway. All the empties make me look like an alcoholic."

"You are an alcoholic."

"I am not an alcoholic. I'm a drunkard." My dad had often made that distinction.

"What's the difference?"

"An alcoholic drinks because he needs to; a drunkard drinks because he wants to."

She wasn't amused. "I haven't made anything for dinner. The boys are home but they're off with friends. There's cold chicken in the fridge. I have a headache; I'm going to lie down." She grabbed a magazine and headed upstairs.

I was resigned to another night of solitude when Zor's advice came to mind. What did I have to lose?

"Before you go to bed, tell me something good that happened today."

Mary stopped and slowly turned around. The query seemed to catch her off guard. I could tell it sparked a thought as she searched for the right words. "Something good, something good…" Her face softened, and she came back down the stairs. "I heard from an old friend today."

Shocked by the sudden change in her disposition, I sat on the couch quietly, trying not to break her mood. Mary put down her magazine and sat next to me. "Kit called."

Kit was Mary's best friend at college. Her real name was Kathy, which became Kat, which morphed into Kit. I knew her well but I hadn't thought of her in years. The last I heard, she had beaten ovarian cancer and was living in Napa Valley with her husband and four kids.

"We spoke for hours. It was great to talk to her. Remember the time we were at the BU Diner, when we started speaking with Greek accents, doing that skit from

'Saturday Night Live,' cheese burger, cheese burger, cheese burger, no Coke, Pepsi? Remember how the three of us were laughing so hard and then you started to choke, terrifying Kit and I, until you did the Heimlich maneuver on yourself like John Belushi?"

I smiled.

"We were talking about that on the phone today, laughing so hard I thought I was going to pass out." Mary was laughing now, and then her eyes welled up.

"The cancer's back. It's everywhere. The doctors say she can fight it again but treatment would be much more intense. She's decided against it. She doesn't want to feel sick the last days of her life. It could be twelve days it, could be twelve months. They don't know."

Mary's voice cracked. "She called to say goodbye and to thank me for being her friend. Her youngest is just twelve. He doesn't know yet. She's just hoping to live long enough to see him start high school." She barely got those last words out before crumpling into my arms.

We sat like that for a long time. I stroked her hair as she sobbed uncontrollably. It was rare to see my wife like this. She had become hardened over the years, much less feminine. I felt sorry for the circumstance, but it felt good to be the stronger spouse for a change.

My mind wandered back to Zor. He was right. The most horrific news imaginable can be a function of perception.

The framing of the question led my wife to focus on Kit's friendship, not her illness. Could developing a positive attitude be that simple? I was working this through when Mary stopped crying.

"I don't feel like leftovers," I said. "Let me take you out tonight." I changed my tear-soaked shirt and she retouched her makeup.

We were driving towards Boston, in silence, when I suddenly veered off the Turnpike towards Kenmore Square. Mary, lost in thought, didn't notice. I took a left off of Commonwealth Avenue and we were there.

Mary gasped. "Oh my God, it's still here."

It looked a lot cleaner than either one of us remembered but the brightly lit sign hadn't changed. The BU Diner was open for business. We parked in front and shed thirty years as we walked through the door.

The interior had changed little. We sat at a booth with a juke box console. I broke out some dollar bills, but there wasn't a song on the screen we recognized. Mary found that hilarious and started laughing uncontrollably.

I'm sure everyone thought we were stoned. We laughed throughout the entire meal. I started to reminisce and Mary matched me story for story. She was radiant, slipping back into the role of a loving co-ed, even running her foot up and down the inside of my calf as we spoke. I'd forgotten how much I loved her.

On the way back we agreed the restaurant choice may have been more romantic than rational. Chili dogs and fries may work well for college kids but the culinary requirements of older adults mature.

When we got home, Mary went upstairs while I searched the medicine cabinet in the kitchen for antacid. Walking to the bedroom, I heard the master shower going. Sadly, I could not think of any reason for her to be showering so late. When she came back to bed I figured it out.

I don't know if it was the chili dog, the BU Diner, or Kit's call, but that night we made love like we were back in college. Not just going through the motions but truly connected, each of us more intent upon giving pleasure than receiving it. It was the best night we'd had in a long time.

The next morning, as usual, she slept in. While making breakfast, I again thought of Zor. What a strange coincidence, bumping into him at Jake's. I hoped he would be there again so I could tell him how well his advice had worked.

If I'd known then what we were about to go through, I would have packed up our things, put the house on the market, and taken my family as far away as possible from that Haitian horror show.

CHAPTER 10

The next few days found me preoccupied with filing taxes. As a professional money manager, I always had the quarterlies for Brewster Capital tallied in advance, but my personal tax return was never as timely. Thankfully, that year, I completed it with a day to spare.

I hadn't seen Zor since Good Friday; not that I needed to, his advice had been perfect. I just wanted to thank him in person. That opportunity came after dropping off my taxes at the post office. I walked into Jake's and saw him sitting at the bar.

"Put that on my bill," I said to Jake. "Today he drinks for free."

Zor smiled. "I take it things are going well."

"Outstanding." My first scotch arrived. "I still don't know how you did it, but I'm forever in your debt. I just don't understand how we let things get so out of whack. It's only been a couple of days, but I feel like we're balanced again. All it took was a little self-examination and fine-tuning."

Zor thought for a moment. "Geoffrey Hill once said that by the time most persons have reached middle age, they've become so battered and bruised by life's incessant blows that they try not rock the boat, lest the little comfort they have achieved be taken away from them."

I took my first sip. "That may be true for many, but Mary and I have lived a charmed life, neither of us has been battered *or* bruised."

Zor shook his head. "The accumulation of negative energy is both insidious and subtle; it can be as dramatic as genocide or as faint as a stranger's sidelong glance. All negative energy is dangerous until we know how to deal with it."

"Well, I've learned my lesson. From now on it's smooth sailing. No more negativity from me."

"Many people attempt to have a positive attitude, but very few actually succeed. In their effort to be positive they continually dwell on the negative."

"What do you mean?"

"Instead of being pro-peace, they become anti-war. Instead of trying to increase a positive, they choose to decrease a negative. That concentration on the negative ch'i attracts more negative energy. What you sing about, you bring about. The best way to quit smoking is to never start. The best way to lose weight is to never get fat. The best way to defuse negative energy is to never fixate on it."

"Deal, don't dwell." I lifted my Chivas in a toast.

"The problem with the neuron net is that it works the same for negative energy as it does for positive. Neuroscientists have done studies with MRI scans showing that when we have a thought, it stimulates the same area of the brain as when we have an experience. In other words, our brain doesn't distinguish between thought and experience; it manifests the same emotional response regardless.

"Every time we think about a negative experience, our brain processes the information and creates the emotional response as if it were actually happening. When we dwell on negative outcomes, we reinforce the disastrous results. A coward dies a thousand deaths, a hero only one."

I offered a second toast. "To the Bard. From now on I'll be sure to maintain a more positive outlook to life."

"Many people say that, but no one really does it. Negative energy is too pervasive."

"Then I shall be the first." I ordered another round. "The next time negative energy comes my way, I shall kick it to the curb." Zor remained silent, watching me. When the drinks arrived I again proposed a toast. "No worries then."

Zor did not touch his drink but leaned closer. "Tell me, Brick, when do you hear the click?"

"Brick?"

ZOR

"Brick Pollitt...Tennessee Williams...*Cat on a Hot Tin Roof?*"

It was my dad's favorite movie and I knew it well. I looked squarely at Zor and in my best Southern drawl said, "Maggie, you are ruinin' my liquor."

He actually laughed. I don't know if it was with me or at me, but for the first time ever, I heard Zor laugh.

"You say you're here every day after work," he said. "Originally I assumed you were avoiding time with your wife, but even when things are going great you're still here."

"What's your point?" I began to worry about where the conversation was headed.

"Why are you here?"

"I come here to relax, decompress, and think about my day."

Zor shook his head. "You come here for the click."

"I come here for the Chivas."

"Don't get defensive. Everyone is searching for the click—that point where we can actually shut off the negative energy." Zor twisted his hand as if turning down the dial on a radio.

"Of course it doesn't really affect negative energy at all; it just affects our ability to experience it. When we turn the volume down, the signal is still there, we just no longer hear it. When you cloud your mind with drugs and booze to thwart negative energy, the energy is still there, you have just temporarily disrupted its reception."

"I'll drink to that."

"Most people do. In fact the five most deadly behaviors of mankind are a direct attempt to thwart the intake of negative energy. These five common behaviors create ninety percent of all health problems. If we took control of our lives, recognized negative ch'i and dealt with it directly, we would eliminate these behaviors and reduce the trillion-dollar healthcare industry to a few trauma centers and some general practitioners."

"You believe prohibition can save the world?"

"Not just alcohol. Drinking, smoking, overeating, drug use—both legal and illegal—and lack of exercise are all destroying the human race."

"Tell me something I don't know."

"All right, how's this? Contrary to everything we're being told, changing these behaviors will not solve the problem. In fact directly addressing these behaviors, fixating on their negative outcomes, only exacerbates the problem by attracting more negative energy, thus guaranteeing failure."

"Wait a minute," I said. "We're finally attacking these problems on a national scale. Everyone knows smoking destroys your lungs, drinking destroys your liver, drugs damage your heart, lack of exercise increases your blood pressure and obesity promotes diabetes. It's simply cause and effect."

"No it's not," said Zor. "It's Freakonomics."

He was referring to a term coined by Steven Levitt in his book of the same title. It spent months on the *New York Times* bestseller list, and like most of America, I found it fascinating. However, I didn't see the analogy.

"What do you mean?"

"Levitt repeatedly showed instances where society has misdiagnosed the cause/effect paradigm by labeling indicators as causes. Think in terms of the gas gauge in your car. Every time the gauge's needle points to empty, your car stalls out. There are many things you can do to prevent that needle from landing on empty. You can fill the tank with water or remove the glass cover and physically push the needle off the empty icon, but the car still stalls out.

"Obviously neither of these actions helps the car run because neither of these actions will affect the amount of gas in the tank. The lack of gas is the *cause* of the problem that needs to be remedied. The gas gauge is just an *indicator*.

"Now, everywhere you look, someone is lamenting our epidemic of obesity and offering solutions. New diet books are generated as quickly as the ink will dry. Providers of fast foods and desserts are cultural pariahs. Everyone has a theory on how to regulate calories and promote proper eating habits, but improper eating habits are an *indication* of the problem, not the cause. We overeat as a response to negative energy. It's not what you eat; it's what's eating you.

"In fact, all five health-risk behaviors are direct indicators of negative energy. Like moving the dial of a gas gauge, addressing an indicator will have no impact on the actual health-risk cause."

"So you don't think we should teach people how to eat properly?"

"I think people should be more concerned with removing negative energy from their life than with removing banana cream pie from their diet. If we teach people to recognize and reject negative energy, then smoking, drinking, drug use, and all the rest will take care of itself."

I drained my drink. Zor's eyes were fixed on my glass. "Do you recognize the negative energy that brings you here?"

"I recognize plenty. I recognize I drink, not because I need to but because I like to. There's no negative energy haunting me."

"It haunts us all, John. Stress, anxiety, remorse, emotional conflict—these are all by-products of negative energy. It may be passed on from those closest to us or from complete strangers. Its source can be as simple as an inconvenient traffic jam or as cataclysmic as 9/11. Negative energy is dangerous. It's the single most destructive force in the universe."

I swirled my scotch. "If what you say is true, there's little wonder we search for an occasional respite."

"Temporary solutions only exaggerate the problem when sobriety returns."

"Maybe self-medication through alcohol and illegal drugs is a mistake, but a well-balanced dose of prescription drugs could work indefinitely." I was searching for a way out of yet another conversation.

"You're suggesting we live in a soma-induced world state Aldous Huxley's *Brave New World*? Do you realize only two industrialized countries throughout the world allow direct-to-consumer drug advertisements, the U.S. and New Zealand? Can you see the hypocrisy of the United States' war on drugs? It's estimated that of every adult you meet today, sixty percent will have taken a drug within the past twenty-four hours. In America, antidepressants are being prescribed at record rates when no one really knows how they work."

"Maybe drug companies choose to bypass doctors and market directly to American consumers because we're smarter."

"Why does such a smart population make such bad choices?"

"What do you mean?"

"The United States has the highest annual healthcare cost in the world, yet the health of its population ranks forty-fifth. In Washington, they budget over two trillion dollars a year for healthcare and spend less than two percent of that on prevention. To prevent illness you must ignore the symptoms and concentrate on the disease. I understand negative energy is debilitating. I recognize that many people need a drug-induced haze in order to get through the day, but getting through the day isn't enough. Prozac, Thorazine, Valium, and Zoloft can make you functional but they can't make you well."

"So now you want to take on the FDA."

"Of course not. Prescription drugs are not only successful short-term remedies, they're critical. The problem is we advocate these drugs as a lifelong treatment when they don't treat at all, they mask. Instead of treating the source of negative energy, they mask its reception. The original rationale for mood-altering drugs was for them to be used as a stopgap measure until psychotherapy could uncover the underlying problems. The problem is these anti-anxiety drugs work so well at alleviating the symptom, no one pursues the cure. Big pharmaceutical companies have succeeded in creating an industry that masks problems instead of solving them."

"Some things are best masked." I took another hit of Chivas.

"Which brings me back to you, John. Why are you here?"

"I've been coming here for thirty years. I think the better question is why are you here?"

"Very well." Zor turned in his barstool to face me fully. "Why am I here?"

CHAPTER 11

His question wasn't rhetorical. Zor actually expected an answer.

"How the hell should I know?"

"To meet you once in the Public Garden, that could be happenstance, but a second and third meeting here, that's no accident." He was speaking softly so only I could hear.

"You think I'm stalking you? I've been coming here for years."

"No, I think you're seeking me."

I laughed. "And why would that be?"

"There's no way of knowing for sure, but I have a theory."

"Can't wait to hear it."

"John, I'm going to guess you're fifty-five years old."

"Close enough." I didn't want to share too much personal information. "And you?"

"I turn seventy this year."

"Damn! You look younger than me."

"Black don't crack." He smiled and rubbed his cheek. "Besides, once you remove negative energy from your life, the aging process becomes quite mild."

Zor paused as if to choose his words carefully. "I think, like most men your age, you are dissatisfied. You've spent your life in pursuit of sex, money, and power with varying degrees of success. You're now at a stage in life where you feel there must be more. You've started to realize that something is missing, and it makes you unhappy."

"That's where you're wrong. I'm very happy."

"You seem content. Contentment is not happiness. Contentment is a limbo between bliss and despair. You have built a life that is better than it could be, but not as good as it should be. We all deserve true happiness, and you're starting to realize you've settled for less. You're mired in the purgatory of contentment, which is causing a crisis of consciousness."

"Crisis of consciousness?"

"Mid-life crisis if you prefer, but it's much more than that. It's literally when you become aware of your life and take measure. It's the point where each man asks: who am I, why am I, where am I?" Zor leaned closer and fixed his eyes on mine. "I'm here because you're there."

I drank silently, trying not to laugh at his absurdity. "You believe you're here to enlighten me, to give me the answers?"

"I have no answers. At least none you'd understand."

The dynamic of our relationship was shifting. I started to resent his smugness but still played along. "Assuming you're right, this explains *why* we met. I want to know *how* we met."

"It was ch'i."

"Good old ch'i."

"To be more precise, it was like-kind energy."

I had no idea what he was talking about and wasn't going to ask.

"Everything about us creates energy," he said. "Our thoughts, our emotions, our ideas, all create unique frequencies of energy. This energy travels instantly and infinitely searching for like-kind frequencies. When similar frequencies discover each other, they're simultaneously attracted.

"Think of it as a room full of sedentary tuning forks. When you enter the room with a tuning fork and make it vibrate at a specific pitch, the one fork in the room that matches that frequency will also begin to vibrate. All others remain silent, but two frequencies seek each other out. In our world, every living thing emits a pulsating energy. When the frequencies match, the sources attract."

"I'm not sending out any secret frequency."

"Perhaps not on a conscious level, but you generate over 60,000 thoughts a day. Each thought creates a unique energy traveling on a unique frequency. One of your thought frequencies was compatible with one of mine, and we met through this mutual attraction."

Attraction? I looked around. Was Jake's turning back into a gay bar? "Sounds like a Disney movie high on ecstasy to me."

"This isn't cinema, it's science. Energy is in constant motion, seeking its own frequency and choosing the path of compatibility. This energy flow is what governs all things. When Einstein said that $E=mc^2$, he was simply saying that everything in the universe is energy, massive amounts of energy. You're energy, I'm energy, this barstool is energy. The day we met in the Public Garden, your energy was emitting at a frequency compatible with mine. Neither of us knew it at the time, but we were establishing a bond. That bond was confirmed the day I walked in here."

I half stifled a yawn. "I don't buy it."

"Think about it!" he said, snapping me back to attention. "I never walk the Theater District, I've never been to this bar, yet the one time I do both, I meet up with you."

"Thanks to a phantom frequency."

"Why is it so hard to accept the presence of phantom frequencies? There are thousands of frequencies all around us we're unable to detect—cell phones, satellites, TV, radio."

"Those are all manmade. You're suggesting natural frequencies are being transmitted without our knowledge."

"Uranium transmits radiation at a frequency we were unaware of before Geiger counters. Whales communicate at a frequency so low we can't hear it without special equipment. Certainly there are many naturally occurring frequencies man has yet to discover."

"So you think our association was preordained? Psychic buddies?"

"Like-kind energy affects the future but doesn't determine it. The energy created by our thoughts and emotions can increase probabilities, but nothing is preordained. Our lives aren't a product of predetermination; they're simply a collection of probabilities.

"When two frequencies are compatible, it makes it easier for the sources to meet. It doesn't mean they will meet, it doesn't mean they'll form a bond if they do meet. How the relationship develops is up to the individual entities, but the initial attraction is a product of like-kind energy."

CHAPTER 12

I drained my drink, started to order another, but thought better of it. "You sound like my wife. A couple of years ago she read *The Secret* by Rhonda Byrnes. For weeks all she talked about was The Law of Attraction and her new positive attitude. She hung up pictures all over the house and crafted her own mantras. She was convinced anything in the universe could be hers; all she had to do was name it and claim it. She even started watching church services televised from a basketball arena in Houston."

"If you're referring to the Lakewood Church, she could do much worse than listen to Joel Osteen. He's one of the most successful televangelists in the world."

"All televangelists are successful—at scaring people and raising money."

"I'm not talking about money, I'm talking about ministry. Forty-five thousand people attend his sermons weekly; ten million more watch it on TV, and every book he writes becomes a bestseller. His achievements don't come from fire and brimstone, but from hope. I've traveled much in my life, and without exception, the nicest people I've ever met are church people. Joel Osteen and his wife, Victoria, further prove the point. Their success at Lakewood Church is profound, not in terms of donations but in terms of positive energy. By promoting good will and hope, they've created a positive ch'i dynasty."

"Nonetheless, my wife eventually came back to reality."

"The New Thought movement has a lot more going for it than you may realize. It's attracted many clergy, philosophers, and authors who share a metaphysical belief in the power of positive thinking. When you transmit positive energy, the probability of attracting positive energy is magnified. You should read your wife's book. *The Secret* is a great introduction to the mind's power. The only problem was too many people saw it as a path to material wealth when it leads to so much more."

"I'm still not buying it. Our brains are remarkable organs, but they aren't supernatural."

"I'm not talking about your brain; I'm talking about your mind."

"Same difference."

"There's no difference between music and a radio? Your mind is your essence, your soul, and your consciousness. It is your connection to all other energy. The brain is an organ—the most complex organ in the body, but organs are just body parts with specific functions."

"And the mind is part of the brain," I said.

"That's where you're wrong. Consciousness is outside the brain. Think of the brain as a receiving device, like a television set, and think of consciousness as a network broadcast. We cannot experience what is being broadcast without the TV, but the TV has no influence over what is broadcast.

"Our brains allow us to receive our consciousness but they have no input into its creation. The brain and the mind are totally separate. Furthermore, like the heart, it is only a matter of time before we create brains artificially. In theory we already know how to create all aspects of an artificial brain with the exception of consciousness. We know the brain receives the external energy of consciousness, we just don't know how."

"You're telling me that with or without our brain, we exist in a conscious state?"

"That's the meaning of eternal life. Some beliefs call it a soul, some a spirit, some consciousness. The most accurate term is ch'i, energy. Every living thing draws from the same source of energy. Plants, animals, humans—we're all wired differently and use this energy differently, but we're all connected at the source."

I smirked and shook my head.

"Think again of TV sets," he said. "Every TV receives the same transmission but uses it differently based on its own unique wiring. Some show a black and white picture, some show color, some are HD, some plasma, some 3D—same signal, different uses."

"I saw the Amazing Kreskin bend a spoon once. Can your mind do that?"

"Again you mock what you have yet to understand."

"I understand plenty. I understand the mind is part of the brain. I understand that modern science can actually measure thoughts as they form in the brain. Without the brain, these thoughts don't exist. I saw a program the other night where neuroscientists are actually reading people's minds using brain scans."

Zor smiled. "Neuroscientists have become quite full of themselves lately, what with all their fancy new machines. Unfortunately, they're drawing conclusions just when they should be expanding the questions. A brain scan shows the firing of neurons and suddenly they think they have discovered the creation of thought. All they have discovered is where the thought is received by the brain."

I shrugged. "Semantics."

"What about post-death experiences?" Zor asked.

"I don't believe those near-death experience claims."

"I didn't say near-death, I said post-death."

"I'm still unimpressed. It's all anecdotal. I'm sure these people believe they died and came back to life. Other people think they were abducted by aliens or are Christ returned to earth."

"You should read *What Happens When We Die* by Sam Parnia, MD. It makes the best scientific case for post-death phenomena. It clearly shows the existence of a life-state after the heart stops beating and brain activity ceases."

"Why is this important?"

"It's critical to understand that thoughts are created in the mind and the mind exists outside our body. Once you accept this, you can understand the effect our minds have over reality."

"You mean over the *perception* of reality."

"Our minds don't just perceive reality, they *create* it. There's no greater creative force in the universe. It's limited only by man's failure to grasp its potential."

"You actually think the physical world can be changed by nothing more than thought?"

"I know it can, and so do you."

I closed my eyes and brought my right hand to my temple. After a few moments, Zor asked what I was doing. I opened my eyes and pointed to the clock. "Using my mind to move time back an hour so we could continue this conversation. Damn, didn't work. I've got to go."

CHAPTER 13

I concluded on the ride home that Zor was a kook—harmless, but a kook nonetheless. I was disappointed but not surprised. You don't meet a lot of Mensa candidates at Jake's.

One thing that did surprise was the success of his marital advice. Since that dinner at the BU Diner, Mary and I had been on fire. She asked me what had happened.

Not wanting to discuss my new friendship with Zor, I told her I'd read an article on positive energy that said good news sustains a good marriage. A few days later she came to me with her own article, printed off some website, which confirmed the idea of positive energy and suggested an additional exercise.

Every night while in bed we were to share one thing that we appreciated about each other (this sounded familiar). There were two rules; it had to be truthful and we couldn't use an observation more than once.

I readily agreed, believing anything that got us into bed together was a good thing, totally underestimating the power of words. The first few nights were predictable—we appreciated each other's love, support, friendship, etc.—but soon a new nightly revelation became challenging. It took real effort, which made us examine our feelings and share them positively.

Telling the person you love why you love them and hearing them answer in kind generates the most empowering emotions imaginable. Needless to say, this added intimacy worked wonders for our sex life, not to mention the added health benefits. Unfortunately, I *did* mention the health benefits when I saw Zor later that week at Jake's.

Zor seemed taken aback. "What do you mean, health benefits?"

"Studies have shown that great sex releases vitamins, hormones and oxytocin that strengthen the immune system."

"Science has determined that? We are now reducing love to peptides, hormones, and vitamins? The benefits of love aren't internal, they're external. The positive energy exchanged is reinforced and multiplied. The experience is its own reward. Once again, determinism and reductionism are stripping the beauty from life."

Uncharacteristically, he quickly worked himself into a frenzy. "*Gott ist tot*—God is dead. Do you understand what Nietzsche meant by that? He wasn't lamenting the death of some supreme being. He wasn't lamenting the death of universal religion. He was lamenting the death of man's ability to experience God. In the late 1800s the very essence of how we experienced God was being systematically destroyed by science.

"The Renaissance had been a beautiful time, literally the rebirth of classical culture. People weren't just interested in the sciences; they were interested in the arts, music, philosophy, anything that would intellectually stimulate their minds. A well-educated man was versed in all cultural endeavors. Science was but a small part of one's education. In fact where scientific experience directly contradicted philosophical thought, it was believed the *science* was an illusion."

"So much for philosophy," I said.

Zor grew more intense. "Everything *starts* with philosophy. Galileo was a great philosopher of science before becoming a scientist, John Stuart Mill was a great philosopher of politics before becoming a politician, Einstein was great philosopher of physics before becoming a physicist. The strengths of their convictions were formed by the depth of their philosophy.

"Unfortunately, philosophical grounding has become more the exception than the rule, largely due to Sir Isaac Newton. Newton's world view was based on reductionism, determinism, and materialism. Don't get me wrong, he was brilliant in his logic, and the masses ate up his intuitive approach, but what we gained in science we lost in humanity. Newtonian science was a successful alternative to superstition and ignorance, but it went too far, denying the human condition of values and creativity. For three centuries the world has followed Sir Isaac Newton and his damnable theories of reductionism.

"We dare not reduce God to a few cosmic occurrences. We cannot reduce the mind to arbitrary neuron couplings. We must not reduce love to peptides and hormones. Newton may have been a great observer, but his explanations lacked true depth. Just because you've discovered an automobile's exhaust system doesn't mean you understand the beauty of its engine."

I wanted to continue our conversation, but I had to leave. My monthly performance review with Uncle Ernie was scheduled for 9:00 am the next day, and I needed to be sharp.

CHAPTER 14

I held a fairly autonomous job. As long as my performance was reasonable, no one seemed very concerned with my business; no one except Uncle Ernie. When I took over the management of Brewster Capital, he made it a point to schedule monthly reviews. As the second-largest shareholder, he had that right, and there was no way around it.

I assumed eventually he would tire of the practice or die, but he did neither. He was from a bygone day; drank, smoked and chased women relentlessly, all without any apparent health risks. Not only was he enjoying life, I feared he would outlive me.

I was in the office at 8 a.m. Ernie arrived at 10:00 without apology. He doesn't start drinking until noon, but he already had his favorite cigar, a Zino, in his mouth. He walked in, passed the security desk, and entered my office without knocking. "You ready?"

"Let's go." I offered no pretense of friendship. This was a business meeting, cordial at best.

I brought a hard copy of the balance sheet to the conference table. I could easily have e-mailed it to him or his son for review, but Ernie was old school (still wore a three-piece suit), and he liked to feel the paper between his fingers.

I think he just reveled in posturing in my office for sixty minutes. That meeting was no different from the others. He reviewed the numbers silently for fifteen or twenty minutes then asked me a dozen questions whose answers he already knew. I confirmed the cash on hand, income and growth, disbursements, economic projections, number of shareholders, and the overall financial standing—all items he just reviewed in the balance sheet.

When he felt sufficiently sated by his temporary alpha-male role, he closed the books, tapped the cover twice, removed his reading glasses and got up to leave.

Then he directed a final question at me, the only one he knew I could not answer. "What about Kingsley?"

"What about Kingsley?"

My uncle pursed his lips. "I see he's still on the books."

"He's been on the books for nine years, why would this month be different?"

"You know damn well why!" He caught his anger and paused. "John, you don't like this investment, and I don't like this investment. Why are we still carrying it?"

"I'll tell you what I told you last month and each month before that. I'm aware of the situation and will resolve our investment in the Dream Farm, LLC when it's prudent."

"*Pipe* Dream Farm is more like it. It's time you admit your dad was wrong. Like me, you advised him against it, yet you continue to defend his commitment. Too much capital is tied up in this with no return. You carry it in our inventory at cost. Lord knows what it's really worth. A current appraisal would probably reduce its value by a third. Face it, your Dad was wrong, and your loyalty to his memory is compounding the problem."

I don't know what bothered me more, his arrogance or his accuracy.

"I've talked with a number of shareholders," he said, "and they agree, it's time to fish or cut bait. I want this resolved by the end of the third quarter, regardless of what it does to our balance sheet or your father's reputation."

There was nothing more to say. He left without as much as a handshake.

CHAPTER 15

Patriot's Day came and went. It may be a minor holiday throughout the country, but it is significant to Bostonians. Both boys called from their colleges to reminisce about the time we participated in the Concord and Lexington re-enactments. Those were great memories.

I hadn't seen Zor for weeks. I assumed he'd moved on, just another transient. Then one glorious day in May when I walked in to Jake's he was at his usual perch. We both seemed glad for the company. After a moment's reflection, he said, "I've been thinking about our last conversation."

"Sorry if I was rude," I said. "It's just that whole mind-over-matter thing ran out of steam thirty years ago."

"You're familiar with the placebo effect? Placebos have shown efficacy rates higher than proven drugs, medications that are on the market today. When a patient believes he's taking a powerful drug, the *expectation* of results affects the illness."

"The placebo doesn't affect the actual illness," I said, "but only the perception of the symptoms. Patients may delude themselves into thinking they feel better, but there's no evidence that they are better."

"That's been the standard response from the scientific community, but new studies are demonstrating something quite different. In a recent study for depression, one group was given a standard antidepressant, and the other group got a placebo but were told it was that same drug. Both groups reported similar reductions in depression. The drug reduces depression by stimulating specific areas of the brain. This stimulation can be detected by an EEG. What was shocking was that when the placebo group was monitored with an EEG, the brain activity was identical to that of the drugged group.

"In other words, the mind's thoughts caused the brain to react identically to the way it reacted when given the antidepressant. The placebo didn't create a change in the patient's perception; it created a change in the brain's activity."

I took a sip of my drink. "Another explanation could be that the so-called antidepressant mainly functioned as a placebo and neither really did any good."

"In other studies," he continued, "patients suffering from Parkinson's disease due to a lack of dopamine were given a placebo and assured it would rectify the deficiency. Soon their symptoms subsided. Upon examination it was revealed their brains were actually manufacturing dopamine as if the placebo was a drug. The power of thought changed a physical reality."

I shrugged noncommittally.

Zor gave me a jolly smile. "Do some research, spend some time online. You'll find many examples of placebos and the proven effects of thought."

"So you still believe the mind controls the body."

"Without a doubt."

"If you were diagnosed with cancer, would you pursue the best medical treatment available or consult a holistic healer?"

"The fact that you even ask the question gives validity to the holistic movement."

I waited for his answer.

"I'm sure there are thousands, no, tens of thousands of people on earth who are able to secure their health through personal energy. I'm not sure I'm one of them. If diagnosed with cancer I would pursue the best medical treatment available, but I would also do everything I could to tap into my personal energy.

"The question is not medicine versus holistic treatment. The question is when are we going to appreciate the enormous power our minds hold? The placebo effect is a scientific certainty. It is a phenomenon that the medical industry documents in every drug test. Placebo efficacy rates reach ten, fifteen, twenty percent; yet we regard it as tricking the mind. Instead of tricking the mind, we should be training the mind, harnessing the power and using it for self-healing."

"This sounds like a TM class I took back in college."

Zor's face lit up. "In its purest sense, Transcendental Meditation is a perfect way to address this. It allows for personal introspection through meditation. Published studies have shown TM to reduce high blood pressure, cholesterol, and anxiety. It's even been shown to increase lung capacity for asthmatics."

"I studied it my freshman year at college."

"What did you learn?"

"It's not a very good way to meet women—you can't talk to them while they're meditating."

"Why did you quit?"

"They kept asking for money."

Zor nodded. "I studied with the Maharishi in the early '60s before the movement became mired in controversy and capitalism. It led me to Vipassana, a process I practice to this day. It's not just about calming the spirit but understanding what disturbed the spirit in the first place. Most meditations treat the symptoms of disharmony; Vipassana treats the cause of disharmony."

"Sounds like fuzzy science to me."

Zor paused in obvious exasperation. "It's a scientific certainty that energy generated from our thoughts affects our bodies. If you refuse to accept the power of positive energy, you must at least acknowledge the devastation from negative energy."

"You are now saying bad thoughts cause bad health?"

"For centuries it was believed that disease was a product of breeding, what we'd now call genetics—programmed at birth, damaged genes damaged health. Then science concluded that diseases were a result of the environment. Exposure to different stimuli created different results."

"That makes sense," I said. "Smoking causes cancer, high cholesterol causes heart attacks, and—" I waved to Jake for another round. "And drinking destroys livers."

Zor shook his head. "I told you, risk behaviors are just indicators, negative ch'i creates the disease."

"Now you're just being stubborn. It's well documented that smoking, drinking, and poor diet are directly responsible for all kinds of diseases."

"The problem with those studies lies in the contradictory data. Some cultures, like the Alaskan Eskimo and the French, have diets very high in fat yet exhibit below normal cardiac disease. Many people smoke and drink excessively but never develop cancer or liver problems."

"Every rule has a small percentage of exceptions."

"No, for a rule to be scientifically sound it can't be right most of the time, it must be true all the time. The question is not why do smoking, drinking, and poor diets adversely affect the vast majority of society? The question is why don't they affect a small minority?"

"Energy?"

"You're beginning to catch on. Eating, drinking, and smoking are all coping mechanisms brought on by negative energy. Think about it. When people are stressed, they smoke, when they're depressed, they eat, when unhappy, they drink. For most people, these actions are indicators, not causes. The negative energy destroys the body's natural immune system, allowing a simple vice to create a life-threatening disease. The immune system continues to work fine for a very small population which may be practicing the behavior without the negative energy."

"If negative energy is so threatening, why haven't doctors warned us against it?"

"Why, indeed. You're just not paying attention, John. Every disease, every treatment, every cure has one medical term in common: stress. The medical profession has finally realized the importance of stress management, but stress is too narrow a term. People think stress is caused by bad traffic, overbearing managers, excessive debt. Stress is much more. Stress is an *indicator* of negative energy. It arises from the conflicted feelings we have when we allow negative energy into ourselves. All negative energy causes stress. When we receive or dispatch negative energy, we increase our stress levels. Accelerated stress accelerates illness."

I looked at the clock; it was getting late.

"Suppose, for the sake of argument, I agree the brain is different than the mind, thoughts can impact reality, and like-kind energy does exist. What does this have to do with me?"

Zor finished his drink and smiled. "Not a thing, John, at least not yet."

CHAPTER 16

While Zor certainly believed what he was saying, I still had my doubts. He thought of me as a philosophical neophyte, but I hadn't been completely forthcoming.

Throughout the '70s I had pursued extensive spiritual guidance. It was not just Transcendental Meditation. I also studied Erhard Seminar Training as well as Buddhism, Christianity, Islam, and Judaism. Never able to find spiritual grounding, I drifted towards a secular world.

Later that evening, after dinner, I went into the attic and pulled out a box of books from college. The religious texts were close to forty years old, but their subject was timeless. I also found *Zen and the Art of Motorcycle Maintenance* plus three books from Carlos Castaneda.

I'd forgotten how marked up those books had become. Most pages were dog-eared and crammed with personal notes. I brought them downstairs to my den and stacked them on my desk where I could not overlook them.

A week or so later, on a whim, I stopped in at a local bookstore across from my office. Something Zor had mentioned piqued my interest, and I was hoping to find a book on meditation. I went to the Philosophy/Spirituality section in the store and was stunned at the size and scope of its inventory. I didn't know where to begin and quickly became frustrated with the sheer number of choices.

Suddenly I heard a familiar laugh. It was Zor. I peered around the aisle and saw him with his back towards me, reading something he obviously found amusing.

He hadn't seen me yet, and I wanted to keep it that way. I don't know why, but I didn't want to give him the satisfaction of finding me in this section. He blocked my exit so I quietly retreated to the coffee counter in the back of the store, grabbed the *Wall Street Journal*, and buried my head in the paper. As I finished an op-ed piece, I felt eyes upon me and looked up into his Cheshire Cat grin.

"Hello, John."

"This is starting to creep me out. How did you know I was here?"

"Ah, the stalker again. Don't worry, I was down the street and saw you walk in. I thought it would be a novelty for us to talk somewhere other than Jake's."

He showed me two books he was carrying: *Letters from the Dhamma Brothers* by Jenny Philips and *Imagery Healing* by Jean Achterberg.

"I'm going to buy these for you. I think they'll add some perspective to what I've been saying."

"Thanks, but I don't really have a lot of free time these days for extra reading."

"It's funny how people find time to follow sports, politics, and reality TV, but not spiritual consciousness. Please humor me. They're both easy reads."

Sheepishly I followed him to the checkout counter. As we left the store I extended my hand and said goodbye, but Zor continued walking with me.

When we got to my building, I again tried to separate. "Here's my office."

"I know." Zor walked past me through the door. "You can tell much about a man from his office."

CHAPTER 17

I was reluctant to mix business with pleasure, though Zor was neither. If he noticed my discomfort, it wasn't acknowledged. We entered the lobby and walked past security to my office suite. Brewster Capital was the building's oldest tenant by a century, and we had the best street-level location. He stood at my window, enjoying the view for a moment, and then walked the perimeter of my office.

As professional management offices go, I fear mine was a bit sparse. Though perfectly functional, my furniture had little pretense: a desk, some shelving, and a conference table with chairs. The walls exhibited various pictures and displays accumulated over the years.

Zor studied everything as though perusing a museum. Staring at a picture of me and my dad golfing in Bermuda, he said, "I see images of your past. Where are the visions of your future?"

"What are you getting at now?"

"Pictures of you with your dad, your kids, your wife, banquets and vacations, awards. I see where you've been, but not where you want to go."

"They remind me of what I've done."

"Who you are reminds you of what you've done. You should be focusing on what you want to do and who you want to become." Zor continued his examination of my office. "Remember your room as a child? Each wall was covered with pictures of heroes, movie stars, and exotic places. You weren't so concerned with what you already did, you dreamt about what you were going to do."

"I stopped chasing dreams a long time ago."

Zor turned to look at me. "Why?"

"When I was a child I spake as a child, I understood as a child, I thought as a child; but when I became a man, I put away childish things." Where did that come from?

"Children laugh over four hundred times a day," Zor said, "adults less than twenty. There are many childhood things to abandon before you discard your dreams. Give up on your dreams, and all you have left are nightmares."

Zor picked up a framed picture from my desk—Mary, Ed and I sitting in the first car I ever owned, a 1967 Camaro convertible. "Who's this?"

"My wife and my best friend from college. God, I loved that car."

"Never love something that can't love you back."

"Those were good times, I wish I appreciated them more back then."

"Since this picture was taken, you have allowed thirty-five years of negative energy to accumulate. The *times* were no better, *you* were. Everyone is nostalgic for the past because it always represents a time when we had less negative ch'i. Unencumbered by that weight, we long for the good old days, forgetting there's nothing good or bad, but thinking makes it so."

Zor swept an arm to take in the whole room. "Everything here is a reminder of what you've been through and who you have become. Everything you have said, everything you have done, everything you have experienced has led to this very moment of existence. Surrounding yourself with memories reinforces that outcome.

"Every picture on the wall, every award on the shelves, and every memory you relive conditions you to remain the person you have become. While the memories may be pleasant, this daily confirmation prevents any real growth. If you're unhappy with where you are, stop dwelling on everything that brought you here."

"Who said I was unhappy?"

"I thought we covered that already." Zor picked up another picture from my bookcase. "Who are these guys?"

"That's the last full gathering of the Brahmin Boys." Taken about fifteen years ago, it included all twelve of us with our wives. I hadn't studied that picture for some time. I believed only four couples were still together, but when that photo was taken we were the masters of our universe.

Zor put the picture back down. "You know, I too am a Brahmin."

"I'm...not sure you know the meaning of the word."

His smile didn't waver. "Perhaps it is you who are ignorant."

Grateful for a chance to prove him wrong, I hopped on the computer, typed in the word, and read aloud from the screen. "'Brahmin, noun, a member of cultural, social, or intellectual elite, especially found in New England.'" I returned his smile.

"Keep reading."

I was surprised to discover a second meaning. "'In Hinduism, the ultimate impersonal reality underlying everything in the universe, from which everything comes and to which it returns.' How could I never have seen this?"

"We usually see only that which we seek."

"Oh, see, in that sense it's a variant spelling of *Brahman*..." He just kept smiling. I started checking e-mail, hoping he would take the hint and leave.

"You won't find happiness there." He played with a snow globe Mary gave me on our first Christmas.

I walked over and took it from his hands. "You keep telling me I'm unhappy. Maybe we just experience different degrees of happiness."

"No, John, happiness is an absolute. I'm not talking about a warm puppy or a good cup of coffee. I'm talking about true happiness, absolute bliss, total harmony. I'm talking about heaven on earth.

"That doesn't exist."

"Maybe not, but it can." Zor walked over to my whiteboard, took a marker and drew a vertical line down the middle with a horizontal line at the top.

"Let's see where happiness comes from, shall we? On the left, we'll put everything that makes us unhappy and on the right everything that makes us happy. We'll then reanalyze each entry to discover where true unhappiness and happiness lie."

"Only if you promise to leave when we're done. I have to work." I had nothing pressing, but Zor's presence in my business world was discomforting.

I must admit, the remainder of the morning flew by. First we listed everything that would make a person unhappy. We covered the board with reasons like poverty, illness, isolation, depression, envy, abuse, pain, ridicule, etc., actually naming more than fifty causes (eventually I stopped counting), without a redundancy.

We then concentrated on the right side of the chart. That was more difficult. At first I thought to just name the opposite of the items on the left side.

If poverty, illness, and isolation prevented happiness, I reasoned, wealth, health, and popularity should create it. However, upon further examination, that wasn't the case. We determined that specific causes of unhappiness could be removed from one's life without creating happiness.

For the longest time, I was stumped. I could name dozens of things that caused unhappiness but I couldn't definitively state anything that resulted in true happiness. Zor suggested I close my eyes and concentrate on my breathing, freeing my mind to search for happiness. It sounded trite but I played along.

I thought of my childhood, running around in stocking feet and pajamas, home from grade school for a snow day as my Mom baked cookies, falling in love with Mary, the birth of my boys, times spent with Ed.

Zor wrote this all down on the T chart. I remarked that each entry on the unhappy side was a single word while each entry on the happy side was a phrase or sentence.

Zor pointed to the left side of the chart. "There are so many things that can make us unhappy. All of them are the direct result of negative energy. If we erase negative energy from our life, the entire left side of this chart disappears. There are no more entries."

"But still," I said, "we wouldn't necessarily be happy."

He then circled all of the entries on the right side of the chart. "Without negative energy, we'll no longer be unhappy, but we need this to be happy. All of this is brought about by one thought, one emotion, and one word."

He paused for dramatic effect and then wrote it boldly: L-O-V-E.

"Most people spend their life dwelling on the left side of this chart," he said. "They know what makes them unhappy and spend all their efforts there. Ironically, focusing on unhappiness attracts more sorrow. They think if they lose weight, get a better job, or become more important, happiness will follow. In reality, the left side of this chart has nothing to do with happiness."

Zor capped the marker and put it down. "Dan Gilbert, a social psychologist and professor at Harvard, has done some remarkable research in the field of happiness. He cites repeated studies that show people maintain a personal level of happiness regardless of external circumstances. One study compared the happiness quotient between recent lottery winners and paraplegics and found no significant difference between the two groups. Another study in 1956 asked Americans to rate their personal happiness. About 30 percent said they were extremely happy. Fifty years later the same survey uncovered the same results. In those five decades the standard of living, quality of life, healthcare, affluence and general well-being of Americans rose dramatically, yet people's personal assessment of happiness remained unchanged. That's because mankind doesn't think in terms of creating happiness but in terms of eliminating unhappiness."

Zor pointed again to our T-chart. "We spend our lives systematically removing these items on the left side of the chart only to discover the item on the right side of the chart is the prize. That is the crisis of consciousness that everyone mistakenly labels mid-life. It is when we realize we've wasted decades chasing fool's gold. To be happy, all you need is love."

"Zor, the fifth Beatle."

"Think about it. Every time you've been happy, what brought it on? The birth of your son, the caress of your wife, the smile of your parents, all of it was love. This shouldn't be such a foreign idea. We all know this instinctively. Children are incredibly happy all the time because they love everyone and everyone loves them."

"Contrary to your earlier admonishment, happiness *is* a warm puppy."

He answered me straight-faced. "Personally, I don't believe pets can return love, but many people think they can. It's well documented those people benefit tremendously from the relationship. They believe they are receiving the same level of love they are giving. That is a crucial point.

ZOR

For happiness to be all-inclusive, we must give as much love as we receive. The best example of this is the transcendent love between a mother and child. With her love, the mother reaches a state of non-self. She feels no boundaries between herself and child and experiences the child's emotions as her own."

He went on to explain what Buddhists call *metta*, noting the concept is common to all religions. It means caring for the well-being of others independent of self-interest. Absolute happiness can only be obtained from absolute love, loving everyone and everything in a totally selfless way.

"I'm afraid my capacity to love is more comic than cosmic."

Zor smiled. "Remember, energy attracts like-kind energy. The more love you give, the more you receive. The more love you receive, the happier you feel. The happier you feel, the more love you give. This will spiral into a cosmic experience.

"Emotions are amazingly collective. That is why our brains respond similarly to things we experience and things we think of. Thought creates the same emotion as experience. We read a book, see a movie, hear a song, and immediately connect on an emotional level. A feel-good movie, a depressing song, a tearjerking book—these all bring about real emotional responses to fictitious events.

"What we need to do is connect to real people instead of fictional characters. We can do that through the philosophy of metta. We can create total harmony and absolute bliss."

I pointed back to the T-chart. "Heaven on earth is a noble cause, but the left side of that chart needs to be acknowledged. Unless we resolve every entry on the left, the pursuit of happiness is doomed."

Zor thought for a moment. "Excellent." He walked to the door. "We're in agreement then. Good day."

CHAPTER 18

I didn't see Zor later at Jake's, I guess he figured one tutorial a day was all I could take. Just as well, I wanted to be alone anyway. After his departure earlier, I had taken inventory of my office. While concentrating on the remnants of my life, I was continuously drawn to the picture of Ed, Mary, and me.

I did love those days and I did love that car. It was good to reminisce. Although I fear it brought on the strangest dream later that evening.

Ed and I were flying an airplane. I was at the controls and Ed was sitting next to me smoking a joint. We were stoned, totally enjoying the moment. Suddenly the plane stalled and went into a death spiral.

We both pulled back on the steering wheel in a panic but were unable to right the plane. Ed then shoved me out of the pilot's seat and took solo command of the controls. The plane was about to crash, and he advised me to jump out just before impact.

I did so, executing a perfect Joe Mannix shoulder roll. Unhurt, I stood up and watched the plane crash into a jungle, trailing miles of debris. I followed the fuselage intent on saving Ed. Eventually I came upon Ed's parents. They told me Ed was fine, thanked me for my efforts, and suggested I go no further.

I woke up in the middle of the night, drenched in sweat. It was the most vivid dream I ever experienced.

CHAPTER 19

By the next morning I was still fixated on that dream. I didn't want to get out of bed. I wanted to lie there and process what had happened, try to make some sense out of it, but I had a business meeting scheduled for noon and I needed to prepare.

At 11:45, Joshua Kingsley was at my office door. We usually met over lunch, but I anticipated a less than pleasant discussion and thought it best to be in a private setting.

I first met Joshua about ten years ago. My dad was still managing the trust at the time, and Joshua had been referred to us by a distant cousin, who happened to be his neighbor.

Joshua, all of 25 years old, represented the Kingsley family holdings: five contiguous farms that totaled over 800 acres in upstate New York.

At the time, his father had recently died and left him one of the farms. The other four were owned by three uncles and his elderly grandfather. The farms were doing well agriculturally, but lack of cheap labor was a growing concern.

Joshua, while studying for his MBA at the University of Vermont, had developed a new business plan. They would reconfigure the farms as a non-profit organization catering to urban youth, allowing inner-city children an opportunity to experience life on a working farm. The new endeavor was to be called Dream Farm, LLC.

Joshua expected eventually to fund the entire project with government grants and donations, but first they needed working capital. To that end, Joshua was looking for investors.

He came that day offering a 4.9 percent limited partnership, guaranteeing a graduated annual income with a 110 percent buyout after year five. My dad liked the opportunity immediately and instructed Joshua to leave his materials behind for further review.

I wasn't impressed and told my dad I thought we could do better in other markets. He said we might be able to make more money, but he doubted we could "do better."

I got the sense he was on the fence until Uncle Ernie weighed in. Ernest hated the idea, not just as an investment but as a concept. "If those so-called farmers want to raise money via donations, that's fine," he said, "but government grants are tax dollars and I want mine spent differently."

I have always believed it was Uncle Ernie's rancor that convinced my dad to go forward. Unfortunately, for once, Ernest proved prophetic. Dream Farm, LLC was beset with problems almost immediately.

Joshua sold the concept easily, securing ten limited partners within six months. Infighting among the farming principals and poor weather resulted in failure to earn enough money for the first year's interest payment.

As set forth in the final prospectus, insufficient working capital could be augmented by retained earnings at the managing partner's discretion. This resulted in a return of capital, which fulfilled the income disbursement but weakened the overall solvency.

When one of the original limited partners started to question the investment's potential, Brewster Capital bought him out at eighty cents on the dollar. Over the next five years, my dad successfully acquired the other limited partnerships in a similar fashion.

On paper it looked brilliant, but in reality we were buying a white elephant. Each acquisition put us further at risk. I remember voicing my concerns to my dad.

"Noble causes require noble stands," he said, and didn't discuss it again.

The project never got off the ground. With the best of intentions, Dream Farm, LLC was a total failure.

My dad didn't care. He absolutely loved the concept, and the worse it looked economically, the more committed he became. He even bought out the grandfather's position for his personal account when he died. In essence that made my dad the controlling partner.

With his passing, the control fell to me. Over the years, Joshua and I had become friends, but I never developed the love for this project my dad had. He had agreed to extend the guaranteed buy-out date for five years, and that extension was almost up. Joshua came by in hopes of further negotiation.

He presented his case well, but my hands were tied. My fiduciary responsibility wasn't to inner-city youth; it was to the shareholders of Brewster Capital, and I knew it was in our best interest to liquidate our holdings.

Joshua was disappointed. Managing the development of Dream Farm, LLC had been his life's work. It was more than a job, it was his vision.

I tried to console him. "I'm not telling you to discontinue Dream Farm. I'm simply telling you I can no longer support it."

He knew I had every legal right to force the sale. "If you force an immediate liquidation, it'll bankrupt my uncles and me."

I told him I had no drop-dead date but expected him to work, for both our interests, in a timely fashion. Hopefully he could locate a new partner to finance the endeavor. If not, I reasoned, a sale to a development company should make us all whole.

There was nothing more to say. Joshua left, and I had a few things to do before I headed over to Jake's.

CHAPTER 20

I didn't see Zor at Jake's again until the first week of June. I was anxious to tell someone about my dream and thought him the perfect candidate. I took my usual place at the bar and started to talk, but he seemed otherwise occupied and cut me off.

"Are you familiar with the butterfly effect?"

"Isn't that some Zen proverb about the wind from a butterfly's wings causing hurricanes in another hemisphere?"

"It's not Zen at all, it comes from chaos theory. The smallest things can have huge consequences. This explains the paradox of negative energy quite well. The smallest occurrence here will cause the greatest tragedy there."

"Are we back on this again?" I was annoyed at his dismissal of my dream.

"We've talked about negative energy impeding individual happiness, but its destructive power is much greater. Think in terms of cataclysmic events. Global terrorism, ethnic cleansing, mass destruction—they're all results of negative energy, the negative ch'i we accept and emit and to which we are all subjected."

"Evil people commit evil deeds," I said. "Negative energy has nothing to do with it."

"Negative energy is responsible for the greatest atrocities ever committed by man."

"If we all accumulate negative ch'i, why do so few of us act demonically?"

"We're all wired differently. There's no telling how individuals will process their burden until it's too late."

"Come on, we're all responsible for dealing with life's trials and tribulations. Don't try to hand me that Hitler, Mussolini, and Mao were innocent victims of faulty wiring."

"There is little doubt despots like Hitler are wired to display the most abhorrent behavior, but I would never suggest them to be victims. Monstrous people committing heinous acts must be punished. However, much like healthcare, if we concentrated more on prevention than on the symptom, we'd be much better off. If we stop negative energy, preventing it from impacting the mind of someone predisposed to genocide, we stop the genocide."

"That's like saying we should stop putting money in the bank so we don't tempt potential bank robbers. I don't care what happens to these people. Their death and incarceration benefit us all."

ZOR

Zor thought for a moment. "Let's think in terms of pedophilia, one of the worst crimes imaginable. An eight-year-old boy, abused by a trusted adult, is the most tragic of circumstances. That child is a true victim in every sense of the word. Yet we know such horrific abuse creates a person who is more likely to be abusive as an adult. When the victimized child becomes an adult and an abuser, we no longer empathize with his plight. He now is not a victim but a perpetrator, and we prosecute him as such."

"Which is at it should be when he crosses the line from victim to predator."

"We don't have to empathize with evil, but we do need to understand it. I would never suggest we forgive the terrorists involved with 9/11. They should be hunted to the ends of the earth, but we need to understand them. We need to know why they did it so we can prevent anyone from doing it again."

"Maybe we should just kill them all and let God sort it out."

"Exactly my point! Negative ch'i. The thought of 9/11 created more negative ch'i, 'let's kill them all'. We have to realize we cannot end war through war, we cannot end aggression with aggression, and we cannot end negative energy with negative energy. Negative energy *attracts* negative energy. Negative actions are the result of negative energy. If we eliminate negative energy, we eliminate negative deeds. Every negative thought contributes to negative energy."

"I understand locking up a child abuser today prevents the creation of a new abuser tomorrow," I said, "but how does a negative thought at Jake's contribute to genocide in Africa?"

"The butterfly effect. Not every butterfly affects the world's weather patterns, but one just might. Not every negative thought causes a catastrophe, but any single negative thought could. There's no way of knowing which piece of negative energy will ultimately be responsible. Therefore we must strive to eliminate it all."

I drank quietly.

"Think of it as a chain of cause and effect transporting negative energy," he said. "A child is beaten by a parent, who was criticized by a spouse, who was disrespected by a co-worker, who was yelled at by a manager, who was subjected to road rage by a stranger, who was given the wrong order at a coffee shop. Who would ever believe the wrong amount of sugar in a cup of coffee could cause a child to be beaten six hours later and fifty miles away? The repercussions from that child's beating will inevitably continue the negative chain of events ad infinitum.

"Furthermore, negative energy doesn't have to travel to other recipients in order to multiply. Internalizing negative energy is equally as dangerous. One bad feeling attracts another. Two negative thoughts grow to four, then to eight and soon your entire mood turns dark. This is when people lash out and do despicable things contrary to their nature. More than just being in a bad mood, it is impossible to think or act kindly when permeated by negative thoughts."

"If we internalize our negative feelings," I said, "we infect ourselves. If we pass them on, we infect others. So we're screwed coming and going."

Zor's eyes grew wide and his tone took on a frenetic edge I found alarming. "If you take nothing else from our meetings, you must take this. *Negative energy must be recognized and defused immediately.*"

He paused for a moment to compose himself. "Man's inability to do this is what drove the theories of Sigmund Freud. His psychoanalytical school was founded for one purpose: to deal with the repressive impulses lodged in his patients' unconsciousness. He recognized repression as a dangerous defense mechanism we all use to deal with the accumulation of negative energy. To release the repression from our unconscious, Freud developed the 'talking cure,' a dialogue between therapist and patient."

"Most of his theories and treatments have been debunked."

"The current perception of psychology is not important, what is important is the accumulation of negative ch'i. If we can recognize it and defuse it before it accumulates in our subconscious, we won't have to worry about whose theory of treatment we should follow."

"So what's your theory of treatment?"

"Vigilance, we need to practice self-analysis. Every time we have a negative thought, feeling or emotion, we need to immediately determine its origin and deal with it; deal don't dwell. If we fail in our immediacy we run the risk of transference, erroneously crediting the negative ch'i to the wrong source."

For once, Zor was preaching to the choir. It was a lesson I'd learned as a young father. It involved my two boys, and I have never forgotten it.

They were both in grade school, running around the house one Saturday, creating chaos as only young boys can. For a while I enjoyed watching them play, but it was the first Saturday of the month and I had to pay some bills.

Sitting at the kitchen table, I quickly became irritated at the commotion and yelled at the boys to knock it off. Subdued, they went outside, but the hurt look on their faces caught me by surprise. I thought about what had just happened and realized I wasn't angry at the noise they were making, I was angry at the bills.

I hadn't thought of it in terms of negative ch'i, but it was exactly what Zor was saying. I mistakenly transferred the source of my negative energy and dealt with my boys instead of the bills. For the remainder of their childhood, I made a point of recognizing my emotional state before reacting to theirs.

Misinterpreting my silence for sadness, Zor tried to cheer me up. "There's good news here. All energy works the same way. Small amounts of positive energy can have spectacular results. Back in the early '70s, everyone believed that to impact society, you had to join the Peace Corps or teach inner-city schoolchildren. The reality is that our thoughts impact the world more than our actions."

Zor paused and looked straight through me. "It's not what we do, it's why we do it. Certainly altruism and philanthropy benefit many, but positive thoughts benefit all. Just as negative thoughts create negative actions which create a negative chain of events, positive thoughts provide the opposite outcome. Your vocation, socio-economic status, race, sex, or religion doesn't matter. It's your personal kindness, acceptance and tolerance that create a better world."

"Sounds like you've joined the PC police."

"When did political correctness become a pejorative term? What's wrong with being politically correct? Political correctness promotes civility. Aren't the very underpinnings of political correctness exactly what we teach our children? Be respectful, be kind, show patience, and empathize with other points of view. Why do we classify these practices as weaknesses in adults?

"Do you think the great prophets like Jesus, Mohammed, and Krishna would have found political correctness so abhorrent? Political correctness simply asks people to treat others the way they want to be treated. We don't always know how other people feel. When Native Americans claim they're offended by sport mascot stereotypes, we should change them. If certain minorities find specific language insulting, it should be stopped. As a society, we need to promote compassion, not conflict. This is why we met." Zor regarded me solemnly. "To end negative energy."

I found his last statement to be ridiculously self-aggrandizing, but I no longer had the energy to fight and said nothing. Zor was also silent, seemingly content to let his words hang.

When it was time to go home, I uttered a final challenge. "Let me get this straight. You think we're going to save the world."

Zor shook his head. "No one can save the world, John, but anyone can change it."

I tried not to laugh. "Right here, right now, you and I are going to change the world?"

"If not here, where? If not now, when? If not us, who?"

CHAPTER 21

That evening, Mary asked about the books piled on my desk. I had topped off the stack with the two Zor bought me. Apparently their newness drew her attention. I hadn't yet told her about Zor, not that there was anything to tell, so I gave a vague response about "gifts from a friend" and successfully changed the subject.

After dinner I decided to do some reading. I never read in a linear fashion. I enjoy skipping from chapter to chapter and jumping from book to book. With the six books in front of me I had a field day.

Actually I didn't need to reread the three books by Carlos Castaneda. I was able to skim the highlighted text and margin notes I had written thirty-five years prior. The books chronicled Castaneda's apprenticeship with a Yaqui shaman named Don Juan Matus. Castaneda, an anthropology student, claimed to have been identified by Matus as a "nagual," a leader of seers and portal to non-ordinary reality.

Castaneda wrote in first-person narrative, asserting his books were nonfiction. Controversy dogged that assertion based on inconsistencies documented throughout his publications. At the time, I recalled giving him the benefit of the doubt—the inconsistency was understandable, given that most of his observations were the direct result of a massive consumption of hallucinogens like peyote and datura.

My margin notes verified the naiveté of a college student in the '70s. I frequently noted his observations and philosophies to be "brilliant." I particularly liked his concept of a non-ordinary reality, a dimension that could only be reached by hallucinogens.

Like Timothy Leary and Ken Kesey, Carlos Castaneda believed, and documented, that a higher level of consciousness could be attained. It was not a reality *caused* by drugs but a reality *shown* by drugs: a new, unexplored dimension.

As I reread my notes and highlights in *Zen and the Art of Motorcycle Maintenance*, I was again struck by how whimsical my beliefs had been. The book was a classic tale of Eastern vs. Western philosophy. A cross-country motorcycle trip by the narrator and his friend John supplied the metaphor. John, in the classic sense, is transported by his motorcycle. He has no real mechanical knowledge and views his motorcycle and this trip with cold-hearted detachment.

The narrator, however, is at one with his bike. He feels the engine at work and experiences every nuance of its being. This oneness provides for a much richer experience.

When maintenance is required for the bikes, John becomes frustrated, in need of a mechanic who can diagnose and correct the problem. The narrator, on the other hand, intuitively feels what his bike needs and is able to anticipate the adjustments required. He believes there is no division between ourselves and the universe.

The narrator's young son is also on the trip, providing an audience for his oral philosophies of realism, truth, and existence. The protagonist references Zen throughout the book, showing how rational analysis callously kills the creative spirit. John tries to defend science over spirituality, continually falling short of the mark.

I was reminded how taken with this philosophy we all were back in school. Revisiting the storyline, I found the narrator's assumptions, while comforting to a college student, juvenile. Thirty years of life lessons have a way of stripping away esoteric fantasies.

Flipping through the book, I randomly stopped at a page with no highlights or margin notes. For some reason, I started to read a nondescript passage that referenced Albert Einstein. Evidently he believed at any given moment, out of all conceivable truths, one truth proves itself superior to the rest.

Something about that statement bothered me. I read it two or three times but I couldn't put my finger on the cause of my discomfort until I read further. The narrator explained that Einstein, by quantifying truth in terms of "any given moment," was suggesting that truth is a function of time. As time changes, so does truth. In other words, all truth, in reality, is relative.

I couldn't believe I had never noticed this statement before. I sat there stunned, trying to get my mind around this concept when Mary walked into the den.

She eyed the titles of the stack in front of me. "Are we going to start smoking grass again?"

I laughed.

"Where did you find these old books, anyway?"

"Attic. From our first apartment on Beacon Hill."

Mary thought for a moment. "These were the only ones you wanted to revisit?"

"We didn't have many others, just some texts from B.U."

"I seem to remember a text we used to have. Not an original, but a copy, a copy of an ancient Indian text." I drew a blank. Mary arched an eyebrow. "With illustrations."

A light dawned. "I did see that up there. Why don't I go get it?"

"Meet you upstairs."

I may have lost a step or two since college, but that night I was in the attic and back to our bedroom before my wife had a chance to turn down the sheets.

Back in the '80s, I convinced my dad to invest in the initial public offerings of Apple Computer, Microsoft, Amgen, and Genentech. We still own those stocks, and their return on investment has been astronomical, but the $14.95 I spent for the *Kama Sutra* a decade earlier has been the greatest investment of my life.

CHAPTER 22

The following week, Mary and I went to Bermuda for our anniversary. We go every year. I brought the books Zor had given me but found little time for them. We arrived home on Friday, just before New England was hit with a summer nor'easter. Six inches of rain in forty-eight hours gave me ample time to read.

I call it reading but it was closer to skimming. I got through both books, and for extra credit, I even checked out some websites.

I was surprised with *Letters from the Dhamma Brothers*. I expected this to be about Buddhist monks on the side of a mountain becoming one with the flame of a single candle. Instead it was about exposing violent inmates of an Alabama maximum security prison to the ancient meditation technique called Vipassana that Zor had mentioned.

I quickly discovered the difference between Vipassana and Transcendental Meditation. The former has nothing to do with relaxation or religion and everything to do with self-discovery. It is a boot camp approach: ten hours of meditation daily for ten days. When practicing TM, I found it challenging to meditate for ten minutes.

Notwithstanding the tremendous effort needed to practice such a grueling method of meditation, I felt the book far too biased towards the inmates. The subject matter of the book seemed to center on prisoner rights, human values, and the power of redemption.

Jenny Phillips, with a doctorate from BU, repeatedly seemed sympathetic to the inmates' plight. She not only advocated for the power of redemption but also aggressively argued the merits of rehabilitation.

Those inmates populated the Donaldson Correctional Facility for a reason. They had committed violently heinous crimes against society. My sympathy was with the victims, not the perps.

Imagery in Healing was a much lighter read. It devoted a large section to shamanism and healers, even referencing the works of Carlos Castaneda. Mysticism no longer held my interest, but I found the material on mental imagery entertaining.

Evidently proof of the placebo effect was much more solid than I thought. The question remained, however, whether the placebo effect was a function of the mind's power to affect reality or the brain's power to manufacture chemicals.

Towards Sunday evening, while surfing the web, I even stumbled across a lecture by Dan Gilbert regarding the search for happiness. I wondered how public libraries were able to stay in business, now that the world's information was just a mouse click away.

CHAPTER 23

Independence Day was quickly approaching, and I had yet to discuss these books with Zor. Mary and I were hosting a large pool-party on the Fourth of July, and the Friday before, I took a day off from the office to prepare. I worked a full day Thursday, however, and later, at Jake's, happened upon Zor.

"I didn't know if I'd see you here again," he said.

"Why?"

"Didn't you read that book on meditation?"

"I read a meditation book advocating prisoner rights."

"I take it you're not a rights-of-prisoners type of guy."

"I believe in victims' rights."

"As do I," Zor said.

"Please don't try to portray those felons as victims. It was their violence against society that put them behind bars."

"I know what all schoolchildren learn: 'Those to whom evil is done Do evil in return.'" He paused for a moment, needlessly adding weight to W.H. Auden's words.

"Violent behavior isn't restricted to criminals. It wasn't that long ago that National Guardsmen were killing college students, Alabama police were attacking citizens with dogs, and the residents of Watts were destroying their own neighborhood."

"The '60s was a watershed decade," I said. "Any freedom worth having is a freedom worth fighting for."

"Tell me why a country founded on freedom has the biggest prison population in the world, over 2.2 million, the largest percentage of inmates worldwide."

"If you can't do the time, don't do the crime."

"Do you know there are private developers out there building prison complexes on spec? They have no contracts with law enforcement, no mandates from the state. They simply buy land and build prisons with the knowledge that America's inmate population will continue to grow."

"Is this going to be an anti-American diatribe?"

"I'm not condemning the American judicial system. I'm willing to concede most of the people behind bars have been justly tried and convicted. The question is not whether 2.2 million people have broken the law; the question is why? They may be criminals today, but they weren't born that way. What turned them to violence?"

"Maybe they were weak, unable to appreciate the tremendous opportunity this country offers."

"Maybe a country that offers so much potential for success creates a greater awareness of failure."

I sighed. "What's your point?"

"Perhaps America's increase in criminal violence is due to an increase in negative ch'i and a reluctance to deal with it."

"If that's what Dr. Phillips was trying to get at, she—like most liberals—forgot to ask the obvious question. Why is it violent criminals always find God after they're arrested and never before?"

Zor frowned. "The inmates in this program were violent felons, rapists, murderers, and thieves with little chance of parole. The hopelessness of their prison lives allowed them a freedom few have. With nothing to lose, they were willing to go deep into self-examination. Faced with a hopeless future, they realized the only way out was in.

"While each felon's path to Donaldson was different, they had one commonality. They were all a product of festering negative energy. Poverty, abuse, addiction—all of these contributed to their choice of crime. Without the ability to process or repel the burden of negative ch'i, they were forced to succumb to it. Practicing Vipassana gave them internal knowledge. We see them progress from violent predators to functional human beings benefiting from harmony and inner peace."

"Who cares?"

"The question to be asked is not why care about violent criminals and their state of well-being, but why aren't we pursuing harmony and inner peace as a function of prevention instead of a function of incarceration? If society reached these lifelong criminals in early development, teaching them how to recognize and defuse negative ch'i, would their crimes have even been committed? The books I bought you show the power of ch'i. I'd hoped you'd read them."

"I read both."

"If you had read, *really read*, both books, you wouldn't need to be here."

"I don't *need* to be here, I *want* to be here."

Zor pushed his drink away. "Now you're just being naïve. There's so much negative energy you're unaware of. Talk radio, cable TV, the Internet, and most of our sources for information have all determined that if it bleeds, it leads. They're looking for ratings and discovered long ago that energy attracts like-kind energy. With so many people dangerously consumed with negative ch'i, it's little wonder that the mainstream media compound the problem in search of an audience."

"So now I should stop reading the newspaper?"

"Avoiding a problem doesn't solve it. Besides, there are too many sources to avoid. On your way to work you exhibit an act of kindness by letting a car merge in front of you, and when you slow down, the car behind you honks, and when he passes you a mile later, he makes an obscene gesture. If you're not vigilant at that moment, a new negative energy progression begins."

"Okay, I'll give up reading and driving."

"Are you going to stop participating in capitalism too?"

I held my head in my hands. "Christ on a bicycle."

"Karl Marx decried capitalism as the most exploitive of all political systems. As capitalists, our everyday life is spent in constant competition with our friends, our families, our co-workers. Always judging to see who wins and who loses, letting others evaluate and define what success is."

"It doesn't have to be like that."

"There's nothing more capitalistic in a capitalistic society than money managers and Wall Street. You spend each day exploiting ignorance, hoping to buy things cheaper than they're worth and sell things for more than their true value." I opened my mouth to protest but Zor didn't stop. "Regardless of your feelings towards the proletariat and the bourgeoisie, reconciliation of capitalism and society is a constant challenge to one's moral standing."

"So I can't interact with people, I can't watch the news, and I can't participate in the economy. It seems to me the question shouldn't be why I choose to drink, but how others can choose not to." I took a long pull of Chivas. "Or why I ever stop."

"Negative energy isn't just what's done to us, but also what we've done, or are about to do, to others—and even what we let others do to others. Internal moral conflicts are equally as dangerous. There are so many things we should do, but we don't. So much good we could do, but we won't. The guilt grows and grows, constantly increasing our need to self-medicate."

I poked a thumb toward his glass. "Do you include yourself in that category?"

"Studies have shown seventy percent of all felonies are a direct result of drug or alcohol use. I'm not talking about addicts who rob you for drug money, I'm talking about violent criminals who have to get juiced before committing a crime. They know what they're going to do is wrong. They're conflicted, and the negative energy arising from that conflict needs to be dulled. Felons don't drink for liquid courage, they drink to relieve their negative energy."

"You were born in the wrong time, you should have lived during prohibition."

"There's no question the absolute removal of all alcohol would be a tremendous positive for humanity, but alcohol and mood-altering drugs will always exist in the presence of negative energy. With the defeat of negative energy, alcohol will no longer be needed."

"You really believe that?"

"Absolutely."

"We all have to believe something," I said. "I believe I'll have another drink."

CHAPTER 24

I sat in silence, content in thought. It occurred to me that Zor had again proposed baseless opinion as fact. I had let him get away with that before, but enough was enough. I took another drink and then started in. "You know, the pursuit of peace, love, and understanding is all well and good, but you've become a one-trick pony."

"What do you mean?"

"You continually espouse fuzzy logic supported by anecdotal, feel-good examples. Everything you say is pleasant enough, but where's the beef? Before I shed all worldly belongings, shave my head, and start dancing in the airport, I'd like to see some proof. Show me some cold, hard facts."

"Contemporary science has an abysmal record at proving things like spirituality and positive energy."

"Are you saying your ideas are more séance than science?"

"What I'm saying is that basic scientific method is woefully inadequate. Instead of testing the causes of certain effects, scientists test the *indication* of certain effects."

"I don't follow."

"Back in the '70s, horticulturists discovered that some gardeners had far better results than others—the proverbial green thumb. They would water, feed, and care for the plants exactly as everyone else, yet their gardens would flourish. Upon further examination, it was discovered that these people also talked to their plants, carrying on complete conversations. Soon this became a social phenomenon, people everywhere started talking to their plants, with mixed results. The prevailing theory was that carbon dioxide, emitted with the gardener's breath, somehow advanced photosynthesis.

"Contemporary scientists decided to test this. Doing double blind tests with both live and recorded dialogue, the data proved inconclusive. While it was clear some people had far better results at gardening than others, it was also clear talking had no effect."

I raised my glass. "Another urban myth busted."

"Not so fast. Talking wasn't the cause of flourishing plants, it was an *indication* of the cause; the cause was the caregiver's positive ch'i. Gardeners who talk to plants exude positive energy. The plants pick up this energy and thrive. The existence of the energy is not *created* by talking, it is *indicated* by talking.

"In the 1980s, massive studies were done regarding children's education. One discovery was that children whose parents read to them each night for thirty minutes did better at school. The correlation was unquestionably significant and immediately hailed as a panacea. Educators across the nation counseled parents to read to their children every night, promising great educational benefits, but actual results have been less than stellar."

"I read to my kids every night," I said, "and their comprehension grew dramatically. Anyone who says differently is an idiot."

"What I'm saying is reading to your children wasn't *the cause* of their educational success it was *an indication* of the cause. The cause again was positive energy. Parents who choose to spend time each night reading to their children are the type of parents who constantly provide positive energy throughout the day.

"Conversely, if parents are supplying negative energy all day, forcing them to read thirty minutes each night will have no benefit to the child. In fact the extra thirty minutes' exposure to the parent's negative forces will probably be detrimental."

He was gathering momentum. "More recently, the scientific community has taken on the power of prayer. The medical school at Harvard chose 1,800 surgery patients as a study group, dividing them equally. Researchers told a third of the patients they might be prayed for, but they weren't; a third were told they might be prayed for, and they were; and a third were told they would be prayed for, and they were.

"Prayers were conducted by scores of churches nationwide for two weeks. There were no statistically significant differences between the post-op recoveries of any of these groups. In fact the group expecting to be prayed for did slightly worse than the other two. Needless to say, modern science hailed this as a definitive condemnation of faith healing and the power of prayer."

I nodded. "Eighteen hundred people seems like a pretty significant study to me."

"They studied the wrong thing. The power of group prayer is not in the prayer but in the group. The positive energy sent to an ill person is what heals. When a patient's immune system is weak, external positive energy is sought, but that energy has to be on a similar frequency. The power of prayer is the direct result of positive energy flowing from one person to another over similar frequencies.

"As of yet we can't tell which people are on the same frequency. Therefore the greater number of people praying gives us the greatest chance of success. Remember the tuning fork? The more tuning forks one uses, the greater the likelihood of finding a match. It's the same with the power of prayer. Recipients of group prayer speak of feeling the energy—the positive ch'i. This is why large praying vigils are often successful. The bigger the sample of people praying, the greater the likelihood of finding someone whose positive energy is on the same frequency."

"So you are now saying the power of prayer comes from positive energy and not from God?"

Zor was silent.

"You do believe in God, don't you?"

"Are you asking about God or about Zeus?"

Now I was silent.

"Query any theologian and you'll be told that religion has progressed from totemism to polytheism to monotheism. Frankly, I don't see it. It seems to me there's been very little progress in religious beliefs. Since the beginning of time, man's need for order has forced us to explain the unexplainable. We have done this with various forms of religion, all of which have eventually been debunked. Currently most of the world believes in a monotheistic God. What's the likelihood we now have it correct?"

"So you believe there's no God."

"I believe *a* God, as depicted in the Sistine Chapel, does not exist. Michelangelo did us all a great disservice with that painting. God isn't a wizened old man with billowing robes watching from above. It may be a soothing interpretation for our patriarchal society, but it's archaic.

Do you really think *a* God sits upon a throne in heaven deciding who prospers and who suffers based on the number of prayers offered or candles lit?"

"Not all religions propose that."

"I'm not talking about religions, I'm talking about God. There's an endless debate regarding the social, economical, political, and cultural purpose for religions, but your question was is there *a* God?"

"No, my question was do you believe in God?"

Zor stared at me in silence as if waiting for me to answer my own question. Slowly he began to speak. "You still don't get it, do you?" He waved a dismissive hand at my drink. "If you drank less you might be able to think more."

Under his steady gaze and demonic smile, my heart started to race. A kernel of an idea, a concept I hadn't the courage to acknowledge, started to form. I had a sense of what he was about to say and it terrified me. The hair stood straight on the back of my neck and I found it hard to breath.

Zor pushed his drink aside and got up to leave. As he did so he leaned in my direction and whispered so only I could hear, "I *am* God."

CHAPTER 25

There was nothing more to say. Zor had left, and I sat at the bar, paralyzed with fear, mind racing. I was a basket case. There was a God, and it was Zor. Our meetings had been a test; his oddities, my disbelief, everything had been a test of faith. I was still in shock as I drove home.

Greeting me at the door for our welcome-home embrace (a new custom for which, evidently, I had God to thank), Mary noticed my mood immediately. "What's wrong?"

I had decided on the ride home to tell her everything. I just didn't know how to begin.

"Is it something bad?" she asked.

"No." I held her reassuringly. Unable to find the right words, I blurted out the only thing I could think of. "I've been talking to God."

She looked confused. "You met Eric Clapton?"

You can take the girl out of the '70s but you can't take the '70s out of the girl.

"No, God."

She tried again. "You came home from work all distraught and in a funk because you've been praying?"

"Not praying. Talking to God."

Mary shook her head. "Everyone talks to God. Let me know when he talks back." I said nothing. She stepped back, wide-eyed. "God's talking to you?"

"I'm not just having conversations with God, I'm hanging out with him, in my office, at the bar, in bookstores. He's everywhere."

She tried to smile. "I think it's called omnipresence."

I slumped onto the sofa. "I'm not joking."

"You honestly think God is sitting down and conversing with you?"

I finally told her about Zor. From our chance encounter on the Common up to today's meeting at Jake's, I told her everything. Slowly she took it in.

"I have just one question."

I expected her to question my sobriety.

"Does he look like George Burns?" Then she squealed, unable to suppress her laughter any longer.

"I told you, he's a Haitian dwarf."

The serious tone in my answer caused her to laugh even harder. "You think God is a Haitian dwarf who's recruiting you to save the world?"

Coming from Mary, it did sound ridiculous. "Not *save* the world," I said, the absurdity of it washing over me, "*change* the world."

We both fell over laughing.

After coming to my senses (sobering up?), the rest of the evening went splendidly. Mary had prepared an outstanding lamb shank, and we were particularly tender in bed. As she slept, I thought more of my bizarre Haitian friend.

I never seemed to muster an intellectual clarity when in his presence. Somehow he was able to cloud my thoughts. Lying in bed, away from his influence, I realized again how ridiculous I had been. Zor as God…what was I thinking?

CHAPTER 26

August third was an exceptionally hot day, and the Common was exceptionally crowded. It was the Boston Hempfest. Usually held in September, members of the Boston City Council had hoped a change in date would lessen the crowd. They reasoned that the usual throng of college students wouldn't make a special trip into Boston if they were home for summer break. The Boston City Council was wrong.

Thousands of people were enjoying the day, the fest, and the pot. It was like a scene from Woodstock, with ages ranging from eighteen to eighty. Peaceful and festive, the gathering presented few problems. Ed always said, "After smoking a joint, the only crime anyone ever commits is possession."

I stopped after work and watched the crowd for a while. It was great to see such diversity unified in celebration. With my faith in humanity restored, I continued to Jake's. I hadn't seen Zor since his declaration of divinity, but every time I recalled that day, I did so with a smile.

I didn't know when I would see him again but was certain he would show up. I got the sense he enjoyed talking as much as I enjoyed listening.

Jake's was totally empty. Evidently the Hempfest had proven a great attraction for others as well. Jake was polishing glasses as I sat and pulled my stool to the bar. Before I could order, I heard a voice.

"Hello, Jonathan, how have you been?"

Zor. I spun around but he was nowhere to be seen.

"I haven't heard many prayers lately. Have you forgotten our last discussion? Have you forgotten who I am?"

Jake continued polishing the glassware oblivious to Zor's booming voice.

"I'm talking to you, John. Don't look to Jake for help. You're the only one who can hear me."

I concentrated on my breathing as I surveyed the scene. Where the hell was he? I didn't know whether to run or kneel.

Jake made an odd noise, and his face contorted as if he were wrestling with an inner demon. Then he doubled over in laughter as Zor crawled out from behind the bar.

My relief at discovering the ruse was quickly replaced with anger at being humiliated. "How long have you two been planning this?"

"Don't blame Jake," Zor said. "I just thought of it when I saw you coming in."

"I don't come here for the practical jokes."

"I'm sorry, but the last time we spoke, you seemed so distraught, I felt I needed to do something to lighten the mood."

Jake, still laughing, brought us both a drink. "This one's on the house, guys."

Composure returning, I looked at Zor. "To be honest, the whole God thing really had me going. It took me a while to figure out you were kidding."

"Kidding about what? I am God."

"Knock it off. Then, it was a funny joke; now, it just sounds stupid."

"I rarely joke, I never lie, and no one has ever thought me stupid."

The game had gone stale, and I decided to concentrate on my drink. When finished, I motioned to Jake. "Can I get a glass of water so God here can change it to wine? Or are you above parlor tricks?"

"I told you last time, you've got to stop worshiping Greek mythology. God is not sitting on a throne with flowing robes and a grey beard. God is energy; God is the life force of all things. I am God because God is me. You are God, Jake is God, and your wife is God. Every living thing is God because God is the source of all living energy. God is the collective consciousness of all living things."

"Do us all a favor. Next time you order pizza, forget the mushrooms."

"I'm not hallucinating. It's quite obvious when you think about it. How many religions refer to God as the light? When Moses spoke to God he saw a blinding light, which he clumsily described as a burning bush. Buddhists pray to the light of Dharma. Muslims believe the forces of nature became active because of the presence of angels that God created from light. Jesus said, 'I am the light'. All post-death experiences, worldwide, spanning every culture and religion, talk of a bright light. This is not a metaphor but reality. God is that light.

"This is the one unifying fact of existence. Regardless of which religious prophet you choose to follow, all paths lead to this light. We are all communal recipients of that light. We are God and God is us."

"Then why don't we all practice the same religion?"

"Hubris. We isolate *our* religious prophets, identifying them with *our* God, instead of accepting all prophets as equals, leading to the same God."

"I'd like to believe this, but I will definitely be very annoyed if I die one day and find you're mistaken."

"Not to worry. You're God, remember? You can't die. Regardless of what happens to your body, your life force remains. Your existence is eternal."

ZOR

"I don't believe in reincarnation. It doesn't make sense. How can a world-wide population numbering in the billions have grown from the reincarnation of an initial population numbering a few thousand?"

"I'm not suggesting reincarnation, at least not in the classic sense. God, the source, ch'i, whatever you choose to call it, is energy transmitted to our bodies. Remember, our bodies are created to pick up the energy like a TV gets a transmitted signal. Each set rebroadcasts the signal in its own unique fashion. There's no limit to the number of sets that can be added. The television set may die, as we call it, but the broadcast lives forever."

"Are you trying to create a new religion?"

"On the contrary, I'm supporting every religion known to man. The prophets we follow—Jesus, Moses, Buddha, Muhammad, even Ron Hubbard, Mary Baker Eddy, and Joseph Smith—may tread a different path, but they all lead us to the same light."

"You speak of Scientology, Christian Science, and the Mormon Church as though they're credible."

"Who are we to judge? Let smaller minds get caught up in the idiosyncrasies of individual religions. Each prophet may develop a unique voice, but the prophets aren't the deity, only the guides. The problem with organized religion is each sect chooses to worship the prophet instead of the prophet's path, which all lead us to the same light, the same source, the same God, because we all belong to the same ch'i. Carl Jung referred to it as the collective unconscious. He felt this was unique to mankind and could be experienced wherever people congregated—churches, hospitals, political rallies, insane asylums, the stock exchange, etc. Pavlov proved a connection exists not just between men, but between all forms of life."

"He proved all that with slobbering dogs?"

"No, he used rats."

CHAPTER 27

"It's quite remarkable," Zor said. "After his considerable success proving conditioned response with salivating dogs, Pavlov started working with lab rats. He designed a maze and taught the rats to seek food at the sound of a bell. Initially it took about 300 attempts before the rats mastered the task. Their offspring however managed the maze in about 100 attempts. The third generation was able to do it in thirty, and the fourth succeeding after ten.

"The progression was even more remarkable when you realize that no two generations were ever in the presence of the maze at the same time. In other words, the parents were never given the opportunity to teach their children how to conquer the maze."

"So Pavlov's suggesting they inherited a gene of knowledge that passed on the required information?"

Zor nodded. "Even though science has determined that acquired traits cannot be passed down from generation to generation; that would have been a logical conclusion if not for the control group. Pavlov found his control group, rats that had no relation to the ones in the maze, showed the same progression."

"What? How?"

"Pavlov found while each related generation of rats had a quicker comprehension of the maze, so did each non-related generation. Rats that had both no direct experience with the maze and no genetic lineage with maze-experienced rats showed the same generational improvement. He concluded that the rats weren't inheriting a knowledge gene but participating in a general level of collective consciousness. As each rat learned how to traverse the maze, that knowledge was somehow shared, *cosmically*, with all other rats."

"Cosmically? That's ridiculous."

"No, that's science. I'm speaking of a well-documented experiment that has been performed repeatedly. This explains what happened in Japan, on the island of Kashima, in 1952. There was a new resort hotel being built along the waterfront. After lunch, the construction workers would feed a band of local monkeys by throwing their leftovers on the beach. The monkeys eagerly devoured every scrap, but eventually realized that washing the sand off the food made it much more palatable.

"Soon all the monkeys in the immediate area washed their food, all their food, before eating. An anthropologist on the island noticed something peculiar. Monkeys deep in the rain forest, far from the sandy beaches, also started washing their food, for no apparent reason. Furthermore, he couldn't understand how the beach monkeys had taught the behavior to the rain forest monkeys since there'd been no direct contact between the two groups.

"Unable to comprehend the situation, this anthropologist called a colleague on the mainland hundreds of miles away and explained his predicament. There was a long pause. The anthropologist on the mainland had just noticed monkeys everywhere were washing their food."

"This is sounding more and more like a campfire story."

"I can only tell you the truth as I know it, John. How you deal with it is on you. There are many more examples of the collective unconscious throughout the animal kingdom, all one has to do is look. How do salmon find the spawning rivers after years in the ocean, or aging elephants locate burial sites they've never seen before?"

"All animals are born with basic instincts," I said.

"We aren't born with basic instincts. We're born with common connections. Instinctual tendencies are not *created* within the body, they are *received* from ch'i. Think of the monarch butterfly, the most fragile of winged creatures. Weighing a fifth of an ounce, sporting a four inch wingspan, newly formed butterflies travel thousands of miles, over land they have never seen, migrating from Canada to Mexico. Science has never been able to explain how they do it because science has always suggested they do it individually. Suggestions range from navigating wind currents, to following electro-magnetic fields, to guidance from astronomical constellations. These creatures have a brain the size of a grain of sand! They aren't able to think or interpret geographic formations. The knowledge isn't inside, it's outside. Monarch butterflies don't have an internal navigation system; they have access to an external collective unconscious."

"This is all very interesting," I said. "But there seems to be one thing absent. If we can find all of these examples of the collective unconscious in animals, why can't we find it in humans?"

"Perhaps modern science continues to look in the wrong place."

"And where does God suggest they look?"

"A good place to start any intellectual endeavor is Cambridge, Massachusetts."

CHAPTER 28

I assumed he meant Harvard, but again Zor zigged when I expected him to zag. MIT is where our conversation went, and to one of its leading intellectuals, Noam Chomsky.

"He's a communist," I said. "Anti-American."

"Maybe a social libertarian, but political activism is the most pro-American stand one can take. Anyway, I'm not interested in his politics, I'm interested in his intellect. Long before he started protesting the Vietnam War, Chomsky was renowned as a linguist. In 1957 he wrote *Syntactic Structures*, one of the most important texts in the field. In this book and others, Chomsky argued that language is bigger than the individual. We're all connected to an innate knowledge or universal grammar.

"This was an astounding concept. Until Chomsky's dissertations, it was thought that all language was learned by experience. What Chomsky showed was all children—regardless of environment, intelligence, or social structure—learned language at about the same time, two years old. In fact, children with severe learning disabilities and/or poor modeling environments still developed relatively competent linguistic skills. If one's environment does not dictate language development, then what does?"

"Chomsky believes in ch'i?"

Zor shook his head sadly. "Like all other scientists, he's looking inside the brain for the answer, but at least he acknowledges some type of universal connectivity amongst mankind. His suggestion that language was developed by something other than imitation was of itself groundbreaking, but he went further. Chomsky showed that the complexity of language, with infinite structure, meanings, and nuances, can only be understood due to an unconscious knowledge we all possess.

"This is the exact problem engineers are having with artificial intelligence. We can develop machines with thinking capacity far greater than man's, but we cannot design them to understand language in a free-flowing conversation. Machines cannot understand or develop a language because they have no access to the collective unconscious."

"Maybe it has nothing to do with external forces," I said. "Maybe at birth our brains are a blank slate, hardwired to develop our parents' language in about two years."

"Why then do adopted children develop language similar to non-biological parents? If you switch babies at birth, giving an English child to Taiwanese parents and vice versa, the children will speak and understand their adoptive parent's language, forsaking any biological preference."

"Then it is imitation that develops language."

"Children with very limited exposure to outside influences still develop complex language and structure at two years old. There is something greater than imitation at work here. Something that guides butterflies to migration, bears to hibernation, and people to conversation."

Zor stood up, paid his tab, and left without another word.

CHAPTER 29

Driving home later that night, I experienced an unsettling sense of remorse. At first I thought it was due to the Hempfest, regretting my lack of participation. Back in the day, I would have been dancing through the night. My angst at getting old was getting old.

But it was more than days gone by and missed opportunities. It was Zor. He was getting to me, challenging my very foundations. There was much he said I could discount, but his take on religion weighed on my mind. It brought into question everything I had believed. I was raised Baptist and naturally accepted Christ as my savior.

Throughout my entire adult life I had been successful at compartmentalizing my religion on a need-to-feel basis. I never really prayed or participated in formal worship. I felt God was there if I needed him, and as long as I was relatively good, I had nothing to fear.

Perhaps my view of God was antiquated, but it provided a quiet comfort. If there wasn't a supreme being watching over us, what was there? The last time I felt this uneasy about religion was in college. Ed was Jewish, I was Baptist, and we had many cannabis-fueled debates.

I again thought of the dream I'd had. I no longer needed to tell Zor but was still gripped by the vividness of that plane crash.

I missed Ed. Ever since the day Zor came to my office, I found myself thinking more and more about him. Over the years I had toyed with the notion of looking him up but never knew what I would say. Lately the conversation seemed less important than the reconnection. Our last conversation was thirty years ago. I wondered if he still held a grudge.

The next day in my office, I entered his name on the Internet. There were over 7,000 results. I continued my search adding personal items like his year of birth, Boston University, and the Peace Corps. Within ten minutes I had winnowed the group down to sixty-eight members.

Checking each one, I finally found an Ed Rosenberg Automotive Center in Zimbabwe. I doubted Ed was still in Africa, and I was certain he wasn't selling cars, but there was an e-mail address, so I sent out a quick message.

Almost immediately I received an automatic response identifying the business as an auto rental shop. There was a linked website, and when I clicked on it, Ed's picture appeared. He had lost some hair and gained some weight, but it was definitely Ed. The contact information displayed an address and international phone number. I had no idea of the time difference but decided to call anyway.

"Hello, Rosenberg Autos."

"Hi," I said. "I'm looking for Ed Rosenberg."

"You got him."

I knew thirty years would change his voice, but I was surprised at his thick African accent. "Ed, it's John. John Brewster."

"Hello, Mr. Brewster, how may I help?"

"Ed, it's me. John Brewster from college."

"What college do you need a car delivered to, sir?"

"I don't need a car. We went to B.U. together."

"I never went to B.U., sir."

How many Ed Rosenbergs could there be in Zimbabwe?

"My dad did, though. You must be looking for him."

I laughed. "Of course. Yes, is your father there?" I hoped my eagerness wasn't too obvious.

"I'm afraid my father passed away about six months ago."

I couldn't believe it. I waited thirty-plus years to call, and I missed him by six months. I was stunned. I think I said I was sorry. I don't really remember; for a moment my mind shut down and went on autopilot.

"You went to college with my dad?" His upbeat tone brought me back.

"Yes, we were roommates."

"Are you the guy with the Camaro?"

I smiled. "That's me."

"No kidding. My dad had a picture on the wall of you, him, and some chick sitting in that car. I always used to ask him about it, and he just said it reminded him of good times. It was the only picture from the states he ever hung up."

We talked for a while. He told me how Ed and his mother, a missionary from England, had started an orphanage for refugees twenty-five years ago. They were married and had their only son within eighteen months of meeting. Life in Rhodesia was hard, especially for whites. Eventually they moved to the capital city, and Ed fell into a car rental business.

Moderately successful, he worked at it until succumbing to a three-year battle with cancer last year. His wife went back to work at the orphanage, and Ed Jr. took over the business.

I told him again how sorry I was for his loss, when suddenly he became quite animated. "Wait a minute. You're John Brewster?"

"Yes."

"Don't hang up. I've got to get something."

I heard him lay down the receiver and rummage through some boxes.

"You're at 2 School Street in Boston, right?"

"How did you know?"

"I was cleaning up my Dad's things, and there was a box here with your name and address."

"You're kidding."

"I have no idea what's in it. Looks like it's a couple years old. I think he knew he was dying when he addressed it. He must have forgotten to send it. I'd be happy to mail it to you, but I can't make out the company name."

"Brewster Capital."

"Now I see it. I'm going to post this right now. It'll go out in tomorrow's mail."

With that we said our goodbyes.

Eight days later the package was on my desk. I opened it slowly. The first thing I saw was a Polaroid snapshot of Ed, Mary, and me sitting in my Camaro. He had written me a note on the back.

"Better to fail at what you love than succeed at what you hate. Good times. Call me."

The phone number was faded. If he had only sent this when he originally wrapped it, I would have called immediately. I put down the picture and removed some wadded up old newspapers from the box.

The gift he had sent showed some wear. An ear had been chipped off and some of the paint was cracking, but it was good to see an old friend. I proudly set it on the bookshelf across from my desk, choking up slightly, remembering the day it was purchased.

My teary gaze was serenely returned by the inscrutable Kong.

CHAPTER 30

For the next few weeks I couldn't stop thinking about Ed. Did he know he never mailed me that package, or did he think I ignored it? The guilt from abandoning a friend resurfaced. I contacted his wife and sent her a long e-mail. It was important that she know what Ed meant to me.

She was gracious and filled me in on his life. For the most part he had been happy, she said, but conflicted about leaving the orphanage. They had both worked there for years, at great personal peril, reluctantly leaving for the welfare of their son.

It never felt right to Ed. He considered it his one failure in life. They had planned to go back when Ed Jr. was old enough to get out on his own, but cancer interceded. It may have been for the best, said his wife. Conditions at the orphanage were deplorable.

Lack of sanitation and hunger plagued all. The government had made promises but kept none. She felt within six months the orphanage would be disbanded, putting hundreds of boys at risk. She closed by saying the orphanage had provided a connection with her late husband and it was particularly heartbreaking to lose him again.

By the twentieth reading of that e-mail I had formulated a plan and placed a call to Joshua Kingsley. Perhaps I was too late to help Ed, but I could still save his world.

CHAPTER 31

Joshua answered the phone himself. "Funny you should call. I was just thinking of you. We've got the property sold."

"What? Who bought it?"

"A contractor out of Arkansas. He buys huge tracts of land and builds prefab housing developments."

"You're turning Dream Farm, LLC, into a trailer park?"

"These aren't trailers, they're prefabricated houses."

"Did you sign an offer to purchase yet?"

"Nothing has been signed, but we came to terms verbally. Our lawyers are drawing up the contract as we speak."

"Why haven't you told me about it?"

"Like I said, we have nothing in writing and I didn't want to get your hopes up. I was going to send you the contracts as soon as they're ready."

I remained silent.

"I expected at least a sigh of relief. You've been on me for years to get this thing sold."

I didn't know what to say.

"Why are you calling me?"

"I was thinking about taking you up on your offer."

"What offer?"

"To buy you out."

Now it was Joshua's turn for surprise. "I've been trying to sell this to you for years. I finally find an interested party and suddenly you want to be in the mix."

"Josh, we've worked together for a long time. I'm willing to match whatever offer is on the table, price and terms."

"I thought you said Brewster Capital isn't in the real estate management business."

"Brewster Capital won't be buying, I will."

"Personally? It'll never work. These guys have made an offer with no contingencies. They're paying cash and will close by the end of the month, less than fifteen business days. It would take you months to line up financing. You just can't match this offer."

"Josh, if I say I'm buying, I'm buying. Give me the time and we'll close this puppy in sixty days."

"John, you're an honest man, and I'm sure if you say you're going to buy it, you intend to. And I know I can't make any kind of a deal without your approval. But nothing is done until it's done. We can transfer title in two weeks. If it were up to me, I'd accept your offer, but you can't expect my uncles to change horses midstream when we're hemorrhaging cash. There's no way they'll put up with a third party queering this deal, especially if it means delaying the closing date."

I thought for a moment. "Then I won't delay the closing or queer the deal. I'll purchase the property at the exact price and terms your uncles are expecting."

"How'll you get the financing on such short notice? My uncles won't accept a mortgage contingency."

"I only need enough cash to buy the shares held by you and your uncles. I don't need to finance the entire purchase. I'll use cash reserves at Brewster Capital to buy you out. Then I'll get a conventional mortgage, personally purchase the entire property from Brewster Capital, and transfer it to my LLC. With any luck I'll be able to do simultaneous transactions."

"Don't you need board approval for such a commitment?"

"The bylaws in the charter allow me to act alone if I feel the markets warrant it. Besides, I'll transfer it out to my personal account immediately."

"It seems complicated."

"Josh, between Brewster Capital and my personal account, I have majority control. Tell your uncles if I don't get this deal I'll do everything possible to kill it."

"All right, calm down, there's no reason to get adversarial. I just want to make sure I heard you right.

You're going to pay the same price, with the same terms, and close on the same date."

"You know the law firm I use. Have your attorney change the buyer's name on all the documents to Brewster Capital. Change nothing else and send it to my lawyers. Come by my office tomorrow afternoon and we will execute the purchase and sale contract exactly as you've written it."

"What are you going to do with this anyway?"

"I'm going to make it a working farm."

"John, it won't work. We're selling because we can no longer make a go of it. It's labor-intensive and no one wants to work on farms anymore."

"Don't worry. I know where I can get a couple hundred workers, cheap."

CHAPTER 32

My next call was to Ed's widow. I told her of my plans to acquire Dream Farm, LLC and how I thought it would be the perfect setting for her boys.

I thought she would like the idea, but I was surprised at her immediate acceptance. She then told me her situation had become hopeless. It was only a matter of time before the orphanage would no longer exist, and she realized my offer provided her with the only means of keeping the boys together.

I was amazed at how fast we were able to formulate a plan, especially since neither of us knew anything about farming *or* immigration. We spoke for close to two hours, rapidly exchanging thoughts and ideas.

I didn't expect the farm to be solvent immediately, but I thought I could subsidize it with personal funds and donations. As the conversation closed, I told her my attorneys would handle everything and she blessed me repeatedly.

At Jake's later that day, I thought of Captain Brewster, and his nefarious cargo. I wondered how he would feel if he knew his fortune was financing Dream Farm, LLC. That thought gave me a bigger smile than usual as I sampled my first Chivas.

I hadn't seen Zor for a couple of weeks, but he had a knack of appearing on momentous days. August 18 was no exception. I was thrilled at his arrival and quickly told him everything. For once, he let me speak uninterrupted as I filled him in on Ed, the orphanage, and Dream Farm, LLC. I even thanked him for his insight, crediting our discussions for my new attitude.

Zor sat stoically.

"Don't you have anything to say?" I said.

"If you're happy, I'm happy. But nothing you've described today has anything to do with our talks."

"What do you mean? Dream Farm, LLC has everything to do with our talks. It's a grand endeavor that will make a difference. You must be able to recognize that. This will change the world."

"I told you before the only thing that can change the world is ch'i. Grand ideas complicate the world, positive ch'i improves it. Why are you doing this?"

"Why am I doing this?" I stared at him, speechless for a moment. "Isn't it obvious? Of all people, I never thought I'd have to explain this to you. Not to you! Can't you see these boys need me?"

"There have always been orphans. Why are you suddenly so concerned with these?"

The calmer he appeared the angrier I got. "I won't let you turn this into something bad. My motivation is not the issue. This is not about the why, this is about the what. The ends justify the means."

Zor's eyes grew wide. "That's the single most disastrous phrase ever uttered by man. Haven't we talked about the butterfly effect? Don't we agree that the smallest things can have the largest outcomes? It doesn't matter what you do. It matters why it is done. You may take on the most altruistic projects in history, but if its inception is a product of guilt and its success is a function of deceit, the resulting negative energy far outweighs any good that may come from it. If you're motivated by remorse rather than compassion, it defeats the purpose."

"My purpose is to feed, clothe and care for 200 orphaned boys."

"Your purpose is to allay your guilt."

I couldn't hold back any longer. "I'm tired of your opinion. You talk and talk and talk, but you don't do anything. I've been listening to you for six months and you're like every politically-correct liberal I know. Your ideas sound good in theory, but I'm dealing with the real world. Life is tough, and to win at it you've got to be tougher. It's fun to talk about peace, love, and understanding, but in the end, it's all verbal masturbation. Actions make the world go round, not thoughts. It's time to deal in reality."

Nodding, Zor chuckled. "Reality."

"The reality is I'm doing a good thing, regardless of the motivation. And until you can prove to me that thoughts are more important than actions, I'll continue to stand by my actions."

Zor finished his drink in silence. Expecting him to leave, I started to feel guilty, but he had it coming. I was surprised to see him order another drink, this time coffee. He stirred in some cream.

"Forgive me if I seem confused," he said. "I thought this had all been decided. I had hoped by now your personal experience with spirituality and positive energy would prove to be self-authenticating."

"I'm not saying you're wrong. I'm just saying I don't know that you're right."

"If you can't believe this on an intellectual level, perhaps you can on a scientific one."

"Wait a minute. You always say science is a negative indicator, woefully inadequate in proving anything."

"I was referring to contemporary science."

"Don't parse terms, science is science."

Zor smiled. "It's all relative."

"That's where you're wrong. Science is the one absolute in the universe. You can interpret philosophy, you can interpret spirituality, but science is black and white."

"I know this is going to shock you, John, but the only things in the universe black and white are black and white. Everything else is a relative shade of grey, even science."

"There isn't a branch of science out there that remotely supports the cosmic sermons you espouse."

"On the contrary, there's a science that not only supports all we've discussed, it proves it."

"Voodoo?"

"Quantum physics."

CHAPTER 33

"I know, I know," I said, "light as both a particle and a wave and so on." I had no idea how I knew that but I was certain Zor would be impressed.

"Ah, the *Reader's Digest* condensed version." He and I were probably the only two people sitting in Jake's who knew what a *Reader's Digest* condensed version was, much less quantum physics. "Quantum physics is much more than wave/particle duality. To understand quantum physics, you must first understand relativity."

"You mean $E=MC^2$?"

"*Reader's Digest* again. Not Einstein's theory of relativity, the relativity of reality. You must think beyond the three-dimensional world of cognitive experience."

"The three-dimensional world of cognitive experience *is* reality."

"That's only our *perception* of reality," Zor said.

"I suppose you're going to tell me machines have taken over in a post-apocalyptic world and we all live in the Matrix."

Zor gave a quick shake of his head. "I'm saying reality has been shaped by our perception. Quantum physics suggests there is no objective world. Reality exists in an interpretive state." He cited an example once used by Stephen Hawking. Hawking began with two people playing ping-pong on a train traveling 28 meters/second (100 km/hr). The ball moves back and forth between the two players at two meters/second. When the ball is served in the direction the train is traveling, within the players' frame of reference, it moves just two meters in one second. However, to someone standing at the station as the train passes, in one second the ball moves two meters and the train moves 28 meters for a total distance of 30 meters.

"I get it, everything's relative."

"No, it's more than that. A third observer, high in space, would see the ball move two meters, the train move 28 meters, and the earth rotate 465 meters for a total distance of 495 meters in one second. The first observer is the philosopher, a positivist, internalizing his consciousness. He believes only what he sees or experiences. Metaphysical speculation is avoided. He sees the ping-pong ball go two meters and is incapable of accepting any other view.

"Standing at the station you have a spiritualist, with a more enlightened approach to consciousness. He recognizes the philosopher's point of view but argues a different perspective. Their agreement is doomed. The positivist will never accept the spiritualist's assertions while the spiritualist will accept the philosopher's premise but require expansion.

"The third observer, high in space, is the quantum physicist. He recognizes the other positions and accepts them both. He then explains his perspective and presents a third correct answer. Both the philosopher and the spiritualist protest, claiming that distance is finite and only one of the three answers can be correct.

"But the quantum physicist goes even further. Realizing that all three observers are correct, based on their point of reference, and acknowledging that there are an infinite number of reference points throughout the universe, he concludes there are an infinite number of distances the ping-pong ball travels.

"In other words the ball didn't travel 2 meters or 30 meters or 495 meters. The ping-pong ball traveled every possible distance imaginable, simultaneously. Oh, and by the way, for the extremely small observer, who is actually sitting on the ping-pong ball, it traveled no distance at all."

I was silent for a long time, trying to grasp his logic. "That is the dumbest thing I ever heard. It breaks every law of physics."

"It breaks every law of physics based on Newton's observation of the macro world, but there's more than one world."

"Oh sure, of course there is. Just how many worlds are there?"

"Three."

Zor explained there is a micro, a macro, and a mega world, all existing simultaneously. The macro world is generally considered man's frame of reference. It's everything we see and experience from atomic structures to the Milky Way. The micro world is the quantum world, consisting of subatomic phenomena. The mega world is infinity, the vast expanse of space and time.

"The problem for science is that Newton's theories don't perform well in the quantum or mega realms. To be of value, science and mathematics must be absolute, but we have found in the very small world and the very large world, the consistency of Newtonian physics dissipates.

"Einstein had a similar paradox in the early 1900s. Newton had done an exceptional job of quantifying gravity, but he couldn't explain how it worked. For hundreds of years the scientific community made astoundingly accurate predictions regarding gravity and its force without any ability to define it. How did the moon's mass affect the earth's oceans without displacing one grain of sand? What kept the planets in a predictable orbit? How did this force travel thousands of miles instantly, faster than the speed of light?

"The answer to these questions could not be visualized in a three-dimensional world. Einstein recognized that and suggested the existence of a four–dimensional world, time/space. Representing gravity in a fourth dimension of curved time/space provided the scientific community a means to envision the unimaginable.

"Physicists are again at a similar impasse. Peculiarities of proofs in quantum and mega physics are impossible to explain in a four-dimensional world, therefore the field must expand."

"You're suggesting five dimensions?"

"Actually, eleven."

"Eleven?"

"And counting."

"That's impossible."

"The impossible is what scientists are seeing in both the quantum and mega worlds. Without the acceptance of additional dimensions, we'd be forced to dissolve all belief in Newtonian physics and start from scratch. Instead of disproving Sir Isaac Newton, it would be wiser to develop theories that include his and new developments."

"It can't be true. Something this dramatic would be reported worldwide. If scientists have discovered contradictions in basic physics, it would make headlines."

"The world no longer puts gravitas on science. When Einstein was alive he was a celebrity, treated like a rock star. The public clamored for his lectures, selling out all venues. Science no longer attracts the mass market. The most intriguing discoveries now are confined to PBS and a few scholarly magazines."

"Like what?"

"In the mega world, it was startling to discover dark energy."

"Sounds like a Black Sabbath album."

"It deals with the big bang theory. As everyone knows, it has been accepted for decades that the universe was formed by an explosion of incredibly dense matter. This matter became the stars, the planets and everything in between. It's also a matter of record that the universe is expanding. Everything in the universe is moving away from each other as would be expected in the wake of an explosion. However, what could not be expected was the recent discovery that everything is moving away at an *accelerated* pace. That discovery was profound."

"How so?"

"Basic Newtonian physics would suggest that the fastest expansion would be at the moment of explosion when the energy was at its peak, after which the pace of planetary expansion would decelerate due to gravity and friction. Since the total energy of the universe was expended at the moment of the big bang, if expansion is accelerating, new energy must be coming into play. The universe is infinite; therefore any new energy would have to come from someplace outside the universe, but the universe encompasses all four dimensions. So there must be other dimensions from which this dark energy emerges."

"There has to be some other explanation, they just haven't found it yet."

"All other explanations have been proven false. It has often been said, 'Once you eliminate the impossible, whatever remains, no matter how improbable, must be the truth.'"

"More Einstein?"

He laughed. "No, Sherlock Holmes."

I returned his smile. "Once again you've proven to be very entertaining." Zor gave a mock bow from the bar stool. "But how does this discovery of added dimensions have anything to do with ch'i?"

"It tells us where ch'i is, where it comes from and where it goes."

"You're saying that the universal life force originates in a different dimension?"

"This is consistent with most religions, which portray heaven or nirvana to be in a location mortal man cannot experience. It's the dimension we're drawn to when we leave our physical bodies. It's the dimension in which post-death survivors experience the great light. It's the dimension all great prophets are drawn to. Remember, the prophets are all mortal, mostly commoners, yet they all had a closer tie to God than the masses. Somehow they experienced God on a higher level. Could it have been they approached the dimension that holds ch'i?

"Somehow the antimatter membrane separating us from other dimensions ruptured just enough for their encounter, and once they personally contacted that dimension, they were changed for life. Upon gaining enlightenment, they had no choice but to expostulate."

"Mr. Spock, you spin a good yarn, but I thought we were talking about science. I don't know why the universe's expansion is accelerating, but I'm not a scientist. I'm sure the scientific community has a logical explanation."

"None that I've heard."

"I've never heard of scientists believing in extra dimensions."

"Maybe you're not paying attention."

"Maybe you can educate me. Give me one example of an accredited scientist searching for additional dimensions, just one."

"Actually, I can give you 10 billion."

CHAPTER 34

"In a small town near Geneva, on the Swiss-French border, 330 feet underground, lies the world's largest machine. It's 17 miles in circumference, took over 25 years to develop, and has cost more than 10 billion dollars."

Zor was referring to the world's largest particle accelerator, the Large Hadron Collider. Like all particle accelerators, it is based on a simple premise: make two beams of subatomic particles traveling in opposite directions collide at the greatest speed possible, and watch what happens.

The difference in the Large Hadron Collider is its size. It is able to generate a magnetic field 100,000 times stronger than the planet Earth's. This will enable particle collisions to reach energy levels of 3.5 trillion electron volts, much greater than any manmade collisions to date.

"The entire project has been funded by the European Organization for Nuclear Research. They claim to be searching for the Higgs boson and super symmetry, but in reality they're looking for unexplored dimensions. Since 1970, quantum physics has suggested the presence of multiple dimensions beyond height, width, depth, and time. Particle accelerators may provide the first opportunity to prove it."

Zor finished his coffee and pushed the cup away. "Regardless of the speed and force of subatomic collisions, energy should remain constant. If the energy in the particles, post-collision, is less than the energy pre-collision, we have our proof."

I'm a bright guy, but I have to admit I was lost. My distant stare must have alerted Zor.

"Think about it," he said. "Two particles have a combined energy reading of x. After a cataclysmic collision, their energy reading is something less than x. Where did the energy go? Energy is a constant, it cannot be destroyed. If it's not inside the collider after impact, where is it? It must have slipped into another dimension. The force from the collision tore a microscopic hole in the antimatter membrane separating dimensions and a bit of energy escaped." Zor leaned back with a self-satisfied smile.

I started to get it. If science could prove the existence of unknown dimensions within parallel universes, then the very definitions of heaven, hell, and God itself would be open to new proofs and interpretations.

CHAPTER 35

I needed time to process all he had said, but Zor was just getting started. "As strange as the mega world may seem, the micro world of quantum physics provides an even greater paradox. For a century it was believed that atoms were made up of electrons orbiting a nucleus of protons and neutrons at a defined speed within a defined pattern. However, upon closer examination, quantum physicists have found that orbits of subatomic particles often vary, depending on fluctuating energy levels. But that's not the shock; the shock is that these electrons disappear totally. They leave their orbits at one point and reappear at another with no trace of them in between."

"Where do they go?"

"There are two theories. One is that they travel to another dimension, hang out there awhile, and then return to ours. The other theory, the one I believe, is that they travel to the future. They leave our time/space realm when they disappear. We proceed to the future, arrive at the time they have shifted to, and see them again."

"You're telling me quantum physics proves the existence of time travel."

"It's hard to say quantum physics proves anything. It's not structured like that. Quantum physics proves the possibility of things. In the quantum world, everything is possible within a structure of probability."

"Sounds like *Alice in Wonderland*."

"Quantum physics gives us scientific permission to think beyond the macro world. If the only explanation for disappearing electrons is time travel, then we must develop a theory that supports it."

"I suppose you're going to tell me you've developed a theory for time travel."

Zor nodded slowly. "I don't want to lose you, John, but I have. It's easy to understand time travel once we accurately define time. The problem we've had in defining time is that we've always assumed it was infinite with no beginning and no end. Time is not endless, it is boundless."

He reached for a napkin and pulled a pen from his pocket. "Sometimes the most complex idea can be illustrated with the simplest of diagrams." He drew a straight horizontal line with arrows pointing outward at each end and a dot in the middle. "This is how we've always defined time, flowing linearly, infinite in both directions."

I nodded.

"The problem arises when we define a point on the line. For instance, assume the dot I drew represents the moment in time when you were born. According to this diagram, both pre-birth time and post-birth time are eternal; the past and future continue forever in different directions."

"Agreed."

"But if pre-birth time was eternal, you would never be born. By definition you would exist forever in a pre-birth state. Therefore time cannot be endless. It is *boundless*. Einstein rejected time as a straight line. He talked of curved time/space going forward and bending back towards itself like ribbon candy. As we travel along curved time's path we have the erroneous sensation of linear travel. Constantly moving forward, we aren't aware of the folds in the passage of time that send us back in another direction. He suggested where the ribbon candy touched formed black holes that could provide time travel portals."

"Forget about *Alice in Wonderland*, this sounds like an Isaac Asimov novel."

Zor ignored me. "Although form and behavior of black holes are open to debate, I'm certain the passage of time has no resemblance to ribbon candy."

"I'm sure Einstein would have appreciated your correction... Okay, so what does it look like?"

"Billiard balls and onion skins."

CHAPTER 36

I had no idea how much longer he intended to talk, but I knew I needed reinforcements and asked Jake for coffee with cream.

"You must think of time as an infinite progression through a finite space," Zor said.

"That's oxymoronic," I said, "with the accent on moronic."

Zor spoke of the Greek philosopher Zeno, an older contemporary of Socrates, who has been credited with supplying the foundation for modern logic through a serious of paradoxes. One of his most famous detailed the existence of an infinite progression in a finite space.

He suggested all distance navigated to be an illusion. For a man to travel any specific distance, he must first travel half the distance. But before completing that journey, he must travel half the remaining distance.

In other words, reasoned Zeno, if a man wishes to travel a mile he must first travel have that distance, (half a mile). Before traveling the first half mile he must travel half that distance, (a quarter mile). Before traveling the first quarter mile he must travel half that distance, (one eighth of a mile). Then it is one sixteenth, one thirty-second, one sixty-fourth, etc.

Since each remaining distance can always be cut in half, the progression continues infinitely, delaying completion. Yet we know distances are travelled, therefore we must accept the premise that infinite progressions exist within finite space.

"The concept of time works the same way," Zor said. "Time is not endless, it is boundless. It is an infinite progression in a finite space; in this case, that space is a sphere."

I sighed. "Whatever."

"Travel through time is comparable to travel through space. If we were to leave Jake's and travel due east without stopping, we would perceive our path to be straight and forward, when in fact we would be following the contours of earth and eventually end up back where we started. Upon arriving at Jake's we would conclude that we had not walked in a straight line, but instead, traversed a circular path around a sphere.

"When we travel through time, we're traveling on a nondescript sphere, like a cue ball from a pool table. Suppose instead of traversing the earth we were walking an earth-sized cue ball, perfectly white and smooth with no discernable differences. We would start out on our path due east, eventually returning to our starting point, but we would never recognize it. The entire billiard-ball planet looks the same. We would always be deluded into thinking that we were walking forward in a straight line, unaware that we were infinitely traveling on a finite path."

"But time isn't a white cue ball," I said. "Time is an infinite string of experiences. Yesterday I was drinking bourbon, today I'm drinking scotch. I know I'm not where I was yesterday because of the Chivas bottle."

"You prove my point. It's the change in imagery that fools us into believing time is infinite. As we traverse the billiard ball, surrounding images change. We knew when we walked around the earth and returned to Jake's because we recognized the scenery of our starting point; when the scenery changes, like images in time, we are unable to recognize the loop. I don't know if traversing the billiard ball of time takes a billion years or a nanosecond, but I do know when we return to the starting point all the images have aged to the future, deluding us into thinking we are someplace different."

"Then how are we able to slip from one time image to another?" I asked.

"Rather than a billiard ball, think of the sphere of time as a perfectly formed onion, with each skin identical to the one above it.

"Each time we circle the sphere of time, we lay down a new skin, created from new experiences. Think of this as an extremely thin membrane, like that of an onion skin. Each membrane represents a specific space in time. Every time we revisit a space in time we add a new layer; a new membrane of experiences."

Maybe it was the coffee, maybe it was the scent of logical blood in the water, but I perked up. "You've just contradicted your original premise. If you're adding new membranes with each new experience, you're in fact saying time is infinite. It may be finite in a loop, but if that loop expands infinitely outward with each new layered membrane, regardless of how thin those membranes are, then time is in fact infinite."

He smiled indulgently. "Only when thinking in terms of a four-dimensional world. The world of quantum physics has eleven dimensions, and in one of those dimensions all of the membranes combine. In other words, the membranes of experiences we create while traversing time do not pile up on each other like onion skins, they dissolve into each other and coexist in the same space. All we need to do is enter that dimension where all time coexists, and time travel is a reality."

"Therein lies the rub," I said. "Inter-dimensional travel is impossible. Any portal of entry would prove cataclysmic, a huge black hole with gravity so dense nothing, not even light, could escape."

Zor just smiled. "Remember, reality in our macro world is much different from the micro or mega worlds. Quantum physics teaches us string theory. Subatomic strings of energy make up all matter. We do not need huge black holes to meld dimensions. Microscopic tears in subatomic strings could provide a portal for simultaneous existence."

After a moment I had an epiphany. "Look, for the moment let's assume everything you said is true. I still have the absolute proof that time travel cannot exist."

"I'm listening."

"If time travel is possible, why haven't we been visited by the future?"

"We can't be visited by the future because the future doesn't exist yet. The future is not pre-ordained; it is created by a non-fixed set of probabilities, generated through like-kind energy."

"Haven't I heard this before?"

"But now you can see where the positive energy, ch'i, lies. It's in another dimension, one we're connected to but not cognizant of.

"You lost me."

"Remember when we first met? I told you it was no accident, but it wasn't pre-ordained. Our meeting wasn't definite, just probable. Your energy and my energy were in sync. We met through this power of attraction. Many circumstances could have arisen to keep us apart—an illness, a death, a natural disaster—but barring these unforeseen circumstances, the probability was very high that you and I would meet. This is the essence of life. All things are possible, but the probability is for lives to be attracted to like-kind energy."

"So energy only flows between life forms."

"This is where it starts to get murky. In the dimensions we are cognizant of, energy flows between life forces, but we know everything animate or inanimate is made of energy, tremendous energy. It's not unreasonable to think that in another dimension, one that we don't consciously experience, all things search out like-kind energy. The only way to unify it all is through a multi-dimensional paradigm. Remember when we spoke about religion? In order to unite all factions, we had to rise to a higher degree. The same goes for science."

I groaned. "You're giving me a headache."

He pounded a fist on the bar. "Stay with me! I haven't gotten to the most important point."

"There's more?"

"This all leads to the most profound discovery in science, a discovery that explains everything." Zor paused for emphasis. "The discovery is *entanglement.* At the very heart of quantum physics lies entanglement, a law that allows us to unite science, philosophy, and spirituality for the first time."

Zor smiled at my bewilderment. "The web has more information about entanglement than you can possibly read in a lifetime. However, if you want to start with a primer, I suggest Amir D. Aczel's book, *Entanglement: The Greatest Mystery in Physics.* It should put the entire matter in a proper perspective."

Finally, Zor was done. I sat in silence while he paid his bill, gave a nod, and left.

CHAPTER 37

I never read *Entanglement: The Greatest Mystery in Physics*, but the next morning in my office, while waiting for Dream Farm's purchase and sale to be delivered, I Googled *entanglement* and discovered over two million sites. After clicking around I found a number of entries commenting on Aczel's book.

It seemed Zor wasn't the only one enthralled. The reviews I read were extremely positive, though they referenced little about quantum physics that made sense. Most reviews concentrated on entanglement, calling it the strangest phenomena and crux of the book. When two particles are entangled, a change in one instantly results in a change in the other regardless of the degree of separation.

The change is instantaneous, faster than the speed of light, and occurs even if the particles are on different sides of the solar system. Somehow one particle "knows" that the other is changing, and they both change at the exact same time.

Entanglement is the quantum happening Einstein labeled "spooky." He realized a simultaneous change meant entangled particles were not *transmitting* information but *experiencing* it.

After I read multiple explanations, I had a vague understanding of entanglement but little grasp of its import. Still, for future reference, I saved a number of internet locations where both Aczel's book and the law of entanglement were discussed. I wanted to think about it more, but my immediate attention was drawn back to Dream Farm, LLC.

There had been a slight problem, and it had to be handled delicately with no appearance of impropriety. My original intent was a simultaneous transaction. Brewster Capital would purchase the property and immediately sell it to me; however, proper title transference was difficult due to the fact that minority ownership was held by both the trust and me personally.

My attorneys suggested a two-step procedure where the trust would buy out both the Kingsley ownership and my inherited interest. After title cleared I would then go back and buy the property in a personal LLC for a dollar more than the trust had expended.

I was assured the entire process would be concluded in forty-eight hours. Based on that timeframe, I decided not to pre-notify the shareholders. After the transactions were complete I could summarize everything in the annual statement due two weeks later.

I knew Ernie would object to this "wash sale" but it was always better to ask forgiveness than permission. The next two weeks were incredibly hectic, but we completed all due diligence in time and kept the original closing date of September 7.

The closing was scheduled for noon, but I had Josh come by at ten so we could tie up other loose ends. He still had no idea how I could possibly run this property as a farm. When I explained my intent to immigrate 200 orphans as farmhands he was genuinely surprised. His surprise turned to shock when I offered him a management position, with equity, in the project.

"Knowing nothing about agriculture," I said, "I can't possibly get involved in the day-to-day management of a farm. I'll put together the business plan, make sure it's adequately financed, and provide all the labor needed. But weeding and seeding will have to be on you."

Josh agreed immediately with the details to be worked out later.

The actual closing took less than twenty minutes. Paying cash, with no financing component, streamlined the process. Before disbanding, the attorneys made sure everything was properly drafted and signed, carefully reviewing each document.

Unfortunately, they missed the most important one.

CHAPTER 38

I entered Jake's that afternoon feeling particularly chipper. Zor was already there and I couldn't pass up a chance to rub it in. "It's done." I said.

"What's done?"

"Dream Farm, LLC; we closed today and it's all mine, as soon as the deed is registered."

Zor made no comment.

"How can you still think it's a bad idea?" I asked.

"I've told you before, it's not what you do, it's why you do it. The idea is never as important as the motivation."

"My motivation is to help two hundred orphans."

"Your idea is to help two hundred orphans; your motivation is something altogether different."

"Where's the harm in righting a wrong? How can it be a mistake to help others?"

"Remember Metta. It must be a selfless love. The energy generated from hubris, even benevolent hubris, is toxic."

"If I feel good about what I'm doing, it can only put me in a better mood. This will contribute to a positive causal chain. My positive actions will cause further positive actions."

Zor paused, and then spoke slowly, measuring his words. "I know I explained the transference of energy as a causal chain, but that's not altogether true. Energy doesn't just create attraction, it also unites us instantly."

"I did a good thing today, and you're not going to convince me otherwise."

"I told you last time, it's called entanglement, and it explains the most important aspect of life; uniting philosophy, spirituality, and science. There's a dimension beyond time/space in which all things exist in an entangled state."

"You're saying all of mankind is connected."

"It's bigger than that."

"All living things are connected."

"Keep going."

"Everything is connected."

Zor pointed to me in agreement. "The big bang theory tells us everything throughout the universe was condensed into a single point of matter. Everything evolved from that source of energy and everything is entangled via that same energy. Every thought, idea, and action instantly affects everything else. Everything is entangled everywhere. This is all you need to know."

"You sound like a Buddhist."

"This is bigger than Buddhism, Christianity, and all other religions combined. For the first time ever, philosophy, spirituality, and science are aligned for one truth. Everything is connected. Once you accept this, everything else falls into place."

"You yourself said mankind has always had a theory of existence, a theory that was universally disproved by future generations. Maybe the big bang theory will prove equally inaccurate."

"Perhaps," Zor said. "But all we can do is deal with the truth as we know it at the time."

CHAPTER 39

Later that evening I received confirmation from my attorney's office that the title had been recorded and all had gone well at the Registry of Deeds. Just for the heck of it I googled "quantum physics" and found over 8,000,000 entries.

I was in much too good a mood to sit and stare at my computer screen all night, so Mary and I went into Boston for a celebratory dinner. I had no plans for the following day and figured I would have plenty time to revisit quantum physics, entanglement, and everything else Zor was preaching.

I've never been so wrong.

CHAPTER 40

My phone was ringing as I entered my office the next morning. I didn't have voice mail; in the financial services industry, recorded messages were too much of a liability, but I did have caller ID. The president of my bank was calling.

It was 9:10, and according to my call log, he had already tried to reach me three times. That couldn't be good. I had been dealing with Paul for thirty years. It was more than a business relationship; he was one of the Brahmin Boys.

When I called him back, his secretary pulled him out of meeting. That was another bad sign.

"Hi, John, thanks for getting back to me. Your attorney had a courier drop off the docs from yesterday's closing last night. My paralegal went through it this morning, and you're missing a 21E."

"What's that?"

"An environmental survey, absolving the lending institution from liability due to toxic contamination."

"This is a farm, not a dump site."

"I know, but ever since Love Canal, everyone's extremely cautious. Cleaning up contaminated land is excruciatingly slow and expensive. It's no big deal, but you said you were in a hurry. You should tell the sellers you can't go to record until they provide you with one.

"It went on record yesterday."

"You own it?"

"For the time being Brewster Capital does, that's why everything went to your office yesterday. I need to transfer it out of the fund to my LLC immediately. You told me there'd be no problem."

"John, I have no problem lending you the money. I can sign off on the loan without going to committee and get you the money tomorrow, but I can't finance a deal without a 21E. As the new owner, you're going to have to get one."

I said nothing.

"There's a company we deal with that has the fastest turnaround time in the industry. I've referred a lot of business their way. I'm sure they can get this done in two weeks. In the meantime, we can prepare all the documents, get everything signed, and go to record the minute we have the 21E in hand."

I looked at the calendar on my desk. Two weeks would be Wednesday, September 23rd. The quarter closed on the 30th. As long as this was off the books by then, I should be all right. I needed to be able to show the shareholders a profitable transaction, not an incredibly illiquid, losing acquisition.

"Okay," I said. "But please impress upon them the need for speed."

Paul was as good as his word, Environmental Services, Inc., called me within the hour. I gave them all the information I had, and they assured me a speedy resolution. There was nothing more I could do, so I busied myself with Brewster Capital's annual report.

This was the only part about managing Brewster Capital I disliked. I didn't mind rating my performance; I was pretty good at what I did. I just found the actual writing to be tedious. I used the same template each year, but there was still need for unique analysis and explanation. The next week was onerous. I wrote and rewrote the narrative repeatedly. I still stopped at Jake's nightly to unwind, but I didn't see Zor. I assumed he was disappointed in me and sought more supportive company.

The one good thing about the annual report was it took my mind off of the 21E. That is, until I got a registered letter from Environmental Services. It was short and to the point: the first phase of the 21E had failed. A more in-depth investigation would need to be conducted before a satisfactory 21E could be provided. The cost was considerably higher, with a completion date of six to eight weeks.

Devastated, I called Paul immediately and got him out of another meeting. In a panic I read him the letter.

"Don't worry," he said. "This happens all the time. All it means is during the investigation of Phase 1 they discovered something that requires further investigation; Phase 2."

"What the hell could they have found? I'm buying a farm, not toxic waste!"

"Phase 1 is a simple review of town records. It takes into consideration how the land and all abutting properties have been used. If anything draws a red flag, then core samples are taken, and the land is actually tested for contamination."

"What could have drawn a red flag?"

"I don't know. Why don't you call Environmental Services and find out? In the meantime, I'll lock your mortgage rate so you have no risk there. However, there's a loan committee meeting next week. I'm putting together the agenda, and this will have to be added. I'll present this deal to the board personally. Don't get your knickers into a twist. There'll be no problems."

I called Environmental Services and got an explanation. Evidently big farms have big machinery—tractors, mowers, seeders, etc.—all of which need fuel, and each of these farms had underground tanks. Some were active, some were abandoned, but none had been tested for leaks.

In order to get a clean 21E, borings had to be taken from each underground tank location and tested. If any tanks had leaked, all contaminated soil would need to be removed and cleaned. When I asked how much it would cost for decontamination, I was told it could be hundreds of thousands of dollars, but as the potential buyer, I shouldn't worry as it was the owner's responsibility.

I hung up the phone, sick to my stomach. Brewster Capital was the owner. The fund was suddenly at risk and it was my fault. My mind raced. Obviously financing Dream Farm was no longer an option. To get it off the books of Brewster Capital, I would have to pay cash.

I could do it, but only if I liquidated my ownership in Brewster Capital. These were original shares, held since the fund's inception. It would have been the hardest decision of my life. Unfortunately, I didn't get a chance to make it.

CHAPTER 41

I spent the next forty-eight hours exploring every possible solution, with no success. I couldn't sleep. I couldn't eat. I had never experienced such anxiety. Finally I realized there was no way I could transfer the property out of Brewster Capital without liquidating my shares and notifying all shareholders. Resolved to that outcome, I began writing a new narrative for the annual report.

It was midday when Uncle Ernie appeared. Bursting through my office door, out of breath with sweaty brow, he looked to have been running.

"We need to talk," he said, wheezing.

This unannounced visit and his shortness of breath could only mean one thing; he knew. I didn't know how he knew, but I knew he knew.

I decided to play Mickey the Dunce. Mustering a smile, I stood and, in a rare display of kinship, extended my hand in greeting.

Ignoring the gesture, Uncle Ernie walked behind my desk and zeroed in on the bookshelf and Kong. "What the hell is this?"

"African art?"

"Art, my ass, it's a bong. What are you a friggin' hophead?"

I couldn't help but laugh. My uncle sounded like a character from *Reefer Madness*. "No, Uncle Ernie, I'm not smoking pot. This is simply memorabilia from a long time ago." I kept my hand extended, this time for Kong.

He gave it to me. "Whatever's going on here is no laughing matter."

Dread washed over me. Certain I knew the answer, I asked anyway. "What brings you by today, Uncle?"

"Washington Mutual. I've been a member of the board there for thirty years, half of that time on the loan committee." Of course, how could I have forgotten? He had read the loan committee's agenda.

"Imagine my surprise this morning when I discovered the largest loan ever submitted to the committee is a commercial loan for my nephew. Furthermore, the loan is to purchase a property owned by Brewster Capital—a property purchased, unbeknownst to me and the other shareholders, two weeks ago."

For a split second I actually considered faking it, but Uncle Ernie had the goods. I came clean. I told him everything about Dream Farm: my dad's personal investment, my plan for the orphans, the 21E, potential liability, everything.

I didn't expect absolution for my actions, but I had hoped for some appreciation of my honesty. As usual, Uncle Ernie disappointed. "I reread the charter. Lucky for you, you didn't break the letter of the law, but you certainly stretched its intent. The co-mingling of assets is, at best, questionable."

I wasn't going to stand there and listen to my uncle preach ethics. "What I'm doing is a good thing."

"If your actions are so goddamn noble, why hide them? Something other than virtue is at work here. I believe it's a misguided loyalty to my dear brother. You're more concerned with your father's reputation than with 200 *African* orphans."

With his disdainful emphasis on "African," the muscles in my face contorted.

"This investment," he went on, "Dream Farm, LLC, has been a disaster. Illogical, illiquid, and ill-advised. You didn't want this to be my brother's legacy, so you decided to take the fund out whole. Your blind love for your father has put Brewster Capital on a path to ruin."

I listened numbly, no longer certain of my motivation.

"There's only one solution. You complete your purchase. No way will you be able to finance it without a

21E, so you'll have to buy it outright. Your holdings in the fund, at fair market value, will more than cover it."

He attempted a kind smile and failed. "As the newly created, largest shareholder, I'll protect you from any other repercussions."

"If I liquidate all my shares, I'll no longer have standing. I won't be able to manage Brewster Capital." Obviously that was an issue my uncle had already considered.

"Nephew, you have clandestinely put this fund at tremendous risk. I think it's time you moved on. We can air this all out for a vote at the next shareholder's meeting, but why look for scandal? I think it best if we tell everyone you're resigning for altruistic reasons. You've decided to concentrate your efforts on establishing Dream Farm, LLC. This way you leave with dignity while protecting the legacies of both you and your father."

If it were just my reputation, I might have fought him, but he knew I'd never risk besmirching my dad. He had me boxed in. I knew he was right, I had to take Brewster Capital off the hook, but I didn't have to do it nicely.

"Ernie, you're an ass." He was visibly taken aback at my outrage. "You've been trying to grab management of this company since I graduated college. You may have finally succeeded, but let me say one thing. The happiest day of my life was the day I decided to join my father and keep Brewster Capital out of your rum-soaked hands. You're a disgrace."

Uncle Ernie's eyes grew large, his face bright red. Thinking he was about to have a heart attack, I debated whether to call 911 or go for a walk and leave him writhing on the floor. Thankfully I didn't need to make that choice. His cardio event turned into a laughing fit. I have never seen a man laugh so hard in my entire life. He finally regained his composure, cheeks wet with tears.

"Your dad never told you? All these years you thought you were keeping me at bay? You really think I was planning a coup? My god, I didn't want his job then, and I don't want your job now. As soon as the board accepts your resignation, I'm going to make a motion to bring in professionals. Me, take over the fund? Are you daft?"

I didn't understand.

"First I've got to tell you, I had nothing to do with it. I wouldn't have even known if I wasn't in the office that afternoon when your wife called. She tipped off your dad that you were on your way. He filled me in seconds before you barged in. The whole thing was dreamed up by your dad and your wife. She was the one who brought the idea to him."

"What are you talking about?"

"Remember that meeting at Locke's? Two weeks before you were off to Africa? Your dad told you I was taking over the company? He played you like a fiddle."

"I don't believe you."

"Yes, you do. Think back to that day. Do you really believe your wife was too ill for lunch but well enough for dinner? Do you really believe your dad was afraid of me? You think I had shareholder approval to take him out? It was your dad and Mary. They were scared to death of your friend from college."

His gaze fell back on Kong. "They knew if you traveled the Dark Continent with him, you'd be lost. Mary suggested an alliance. She reasoned you'd never leave for Africa if you thought my brother was in trouble. They both claimed they did it for love. I believed your dad, but I thought your girlfriend was afraid of losing her meal ticket." He closed one eye and tapped his nose twice.

I never liked my uncle, but that was the first time I ever wanted to do him physical harm. I don't know if it was his words or his gesture, but at that moment I had an overwhelming desire to punch him.

Instead, I stood motionless and willed the impulse to pass. Violence wasn't the answer. Besides, he was telling the truth. Perhaps at some level I had known it all along. The timing and circumstances of that lunch at Locke's had always seemed suspect, but for some reason I ignored my suspicions. Allowing myself to be duped, I resolved not to ask questions I didn't want answered.

Now, with the truth exposed, I was lost, adrift. Everything I'd built my life on was a lie. I understood my dad, ever the capitalist; he would expect me to sell out my do-gooder ideals. Trading my life for his lifestyle would seem a practical choice. But Mary, my Mary, how could she have thought so little of me? How could she have conspired to strip me of my dream?

Staring straight ahead, I was determined not to give my uncle the satisfaction of an emotional response. He still had my disdain, but my anger had shifted to Mary.

"Time is of the essence," he said. "If we're in agreement, I'll have the lawyers draw up your resignation and meet you back here first thing tomorrow morning."

I nodded in agreement, and he left without another word.

I looked down at my computer. There was no need to continue with the annual report. In a matter of minutes, I had lost my dad, my wife, and my career. I needed a drink.

CHAPTER 42

I sat alone at Jake's for quite a while formulating a plan. I sensed Zor would show up eventually and so wasn't a bit surprised when he did. I told him everything. Recounting Mary's deceit served to increase my anger.

He thought for a moment. "Are you happy with your life?"

"That's not the point."

"Are you happy with your marriage?"

"I thought I was."

"Glad you stayed on at Brewster Capital?"

"I couldn't imagine a better job."

"Well," he said, "I guess the ends justify the means."

Hoist on my own petard. Lest I missed the irony, he drove it home. "You always said all's well that ends well. So what if the people closest to you were deceitful? The outcome is what matters."

I stared straight ahead, nursing my drink when I heard, no *felt*, that voice again. "Deal, don't dwell." It was the same voice I heard six months earlier, the first time I met

Zor at this very bar. But this time I was looking straight at his reflection in the mirror behind the bar, and his lips never moved.

"What are you going to do?"

"I'm going to have a drink." I said as I waved for a refill. "And then I'm going to confront my wife."

"You've already had a drink."

"Then I guess I'll have another. I'm working through something here. Maybe you don't get it: the two most important people in my life betrayed me."

"And you think the best way to deal with this is to confront your wife?"

"I want her to know that I know what she did. I want her to know how bad I feel. If my dad were here, I'd see him too, but he's gone, so it's all on her."

"Damn the consequences."

"The consequences aren't my responsibility."

"That seems like little consolation for a ruined marriage."

"A marriage based on deceit isn't much of a marriage," I said.

"You're going to destroy your marriage in order to save it? There's no such thing as a scorched-earth solution."

"There's no such thing as a free lunch."

"We aren't talking about your lunch; we're talking about your life. After you go home and destroy everything you've rebuilt these past six months, what then?"

"I don't care whether you understand what I'm doing here or not. This is my life, my marriage. I'm going to deal with it as I see fit."

"That's the problem. All you're seeing is red. Have you learned nothing in the six months we've talked? Anger and bitterness has convoluted your logic. You're overcome with negative ch'i. Your desire to rid yourself of this debilitating weight is overpowering. The easy way out is to pass it on to your wife, but it's the wrong way."

"What goes around comes around," I said. "It started with her, it should end with her."

"It won't end, that's the point. Negative energy never ends on its own. It needs to be cognitively defused. You have the opportunity right now to do so. How you react will change the world. Can't you see this is on you?"

My mind drifted back to Dream Farm, LLC. "I don't understand how something so right could turn out so wrong."

"There is no right *or* wrong. Everything is right *and* wrong. Every possibility exists simultaneously, remember? Circumstances don't define outcomes, we do."

"Yeah, yeah, yeah, everything is relative, the results we expect are the results we get, and all that other tripe."

"It's called visualization. Successful athletes have been practicing creative visualization for decades. This was well documented by the Russian Olympic team twenty years ago."

I had no interest in listening, but I knew protest would be futile.

"Four groups of athletes with varying degrees of physical and mental training were monitored. It was determined that the group with the lowest time spent physically training—25 percent—and the highest time mentally training—75 percent—was the most successful. Life is a set of self-fulfilling prophesies. We do get the results we expect."

"I expected Dream Farm, LLC, to be a great success. It turned into a quagmire. You told me positive energy attracted positive energy. All I've attracted with this is grief."

"Perhaps your actions weren't as altruistic as you think."

"I don't need to hear this."

"Maybe now you understand. It's not our actions that attract ch'i, it's our thoughts. The motivation for your farm was something only you can determine, but that motivation has brought you here."

The alcohol was finally kicking in. I drained my scotch and waved for the bill.

"Metta," Zor said. "Love without self-interest. Finding joy in the joy of others is the only path to happiness. That is where positive ch'i originates. That is where you need to be."

"Where I need to be is home." I clumsily tapped my finger to my nose. "The postman always rings twice."

CHAPTER 43

My mind was uncontrollable on the ride home, jumping from my dad, to my wife, to Zor, to Ed, to the Brahmin Boys, to everything I had done in my life—rapid flashes of conscience.

I knew confronting Mary could destroy everything we'd built, but I had to do it. As I got closer to home, I started to tense up. My hands became clammy and I felt a growing tightness in my chest—classic signs of a heart attack. I concentrated on my breathing and tried to calm down, determined not to die, at least not until I received my pound of flesh.

I pulled off to the side of the road with my heart pounding, shut off the engine and searched the glove box for aspirin. Then the most extraordinary thing happened. Even today I can't completely describe it. I simply refer to it as my Zor moment.

A few years back, at the age of 50, I had taken my first cardio-stress test. Troubled by inconclusive results, my cardiologist suggested an angiogram. Regardless of how often I was assured of the procedure's safety, I still approached it with apprehension. The attending nurse sensed my stress and assured me that I would have a wonderful experience. To my complete surprise, she was right.

I tell of this not because of the procedure but because of the anesthetic; it was incredible. Everyone I have ever spoken to who has had an angiogram always mentions the incredible lightness of being they experienced from the anesthetic, a warm glow of peace and tranquility radiating from the IV drip in their arm.

I was experiencing that exact feeling, again. Instead of starting in my arm from an IV drip, it began in my brain. To be more exact, it originated in my prefrontal cortex. I felt a small pop followed by an intense burning.

The warmth spread throughout my body, creating an immediate euphoric state. I had never felt so good. I have no explanation, but at that moment, for whatever reason, I was transformed.

I experienced a single moment of absolute clarity. I saw the negative energy that was consuming me. I saw what it was and where it came from. It didn't come from my wife, my dad, or any other part of my life. It was a separate entity, a foreign body looking to attach itself to my life force.

Like all other parasites, that negative energy could not exist on its own. It needed to feed off me. Once I realized I was in control and the incredible burden of negativity was dependent on my acceptance, I was free.

I suddenly understood everything without thinking about anything. My thoughts no longer flowed independently, they coalesced simultaneously. I felt a connection to life that was previously unimaginable. At total peace and with an uncluttered mind, I experienced complete happiness.

At first I was afraid to move. Afraid if I moved the moment would be lost. Then I realized it wasn't a moment, it was a transformation. I started my car and drove home in a state of tranquility that has been with me ever since.

CHAPTER 44

I didn't go home that night to confront my wife; I went home to forgive her. Entering the house, I realized there was nothing to forgive; the very act of forgiveness would be counterproductive, egocentric.

I had obtained a new clarity, a new appreciation for what was important and what wasn't. What I did that evening was accept my wife. I chose to love her for the person she was, and that decision has made all the difference in the world.

She could tell something was wrong the minute I walked into the room. I led her to the den, gliding more than walking, and we talked. I told her of my plans to leave Brewster Capital, filling her in on my new connection with Ed's family and my folly at financing the Dream Farm, LLC. The story seemed far less dramatic in its telling.

"I planned to employ Joshua Kingsley as the on-site manager and run the program from School Street, but things have gotten a little more complicated, and Ernie is allowing me to resign."

"Did Zor put you up to this?"

I was surprised she remembered his name. We only talked about him once. "No, in fact he was dead set against it."

Mary reached out and took my hand. "Are we going to be okay?"

I was touched by her tenderness. "We aren't as wealthy as we were before, but when the dust settles, we'll be far from poor."

"No," she said. "I mean you and I, are we going to be okay?"

Feeling a love stronger than I could ever have imagined, I smiled. "You and I couldn't be better."

CHAPTER 45

The next morning I was up and at it early. Letting Mary sleep, I dressed quietly and was out the door by 6 a.m. It was the last week of daylight saving time and the sun was just coming up.

I couldn't understand why I felt so well rested. My entire body was energized, five senses firing in unison. I was sincerely looking forward to the day's events.

In town, I parked my car and walked past my office into the Public Garden. It was a glorious fall day. Serendipitously I realized I had taken a seat at the exact same spot where I first saw Zor six months earlier. Six months? Had I really only known him six months?

I Looked up and could almost see him gliding past the Duck Pond like he did the first time we met last spring. Then I realized I was seeing him. Somehow I wasn't surprised.

"Hello, John."

"Hi."

"Come here often?"

We both laughed.

"How'd you know I'd be here?"

"I didn't."

I found that hard to believe. "Why are you here, then?"

"I thought I would enjoy one last walk around the city."

"Going somewhere?"

A gaggle of geese noisily flew overhead. Zor looked up at them. "When birds start forming in chevron flight, I know it's time to go home."

"Back to Haiti?"

"Yes."

"When do you leave?"

"Sometime today, I imagine. I haven't checked the flights, but when one becomes available, I think I'll be on it."

I smiled.

"You seem calmer today than the last time we spoke," he said.

"I'm in a better place today."

We both fell silent, enjoying the moment.

When he got up to leave, I said, "Will I see you again?"

"Perhaps." He extended his hand. "Goodbye, John."

I shook it warmly. "Goodbye, Zor. I hope you find happiness in Haiti."

ZOR

After a few steps, he turned around and spoke to me for what we both thought would be the last time. "Happiness isn't in the destination, John, it's in the journey."

CHAPTER 46

I watched him disappear beyond the swan boats, surprised by my lack of melancholy. I guess I always knew he was a free spirit, and frankly, even if he stayed in Boston, I could never be sure of seeing him again. I sat there a while longer, amazed at how much he taught me and how little I knew about him.

The chimes from the Park Street Church alerted me to the time. Uncle Ernie would be waiting. I sped to my office feeling much like George Bailey at the end of *It's a Wonderful Life,* happily walking towards an outcome that would have been unthinkable forty-eight hours prior.

I was wrong, Uncle Ernie wasn't waiting; he was already in my office with a locksmith changing the lock. I smiled at his eagerness and shook his hand warmly. If surprised by my demeanor, he didn't let on.

Our attorneys were both there and I signed everything within thirty minutes. I took a few personal things and told Ernie anything he didn't want he could ship to my house. I could tell everyone felt uncomfortable so I left quickly.

On the way back to my car I passed Jake's as it opened for lunch. Surprisingly, I had no interest in going in. I wanted to get home to my wife and share the two items I had rescued from my office: a picture of three college kids in a yellow Camaro and a ceramic figurine of King Kong.

THE ENDING

I did see Zor one more time. Ten months later in the middle of summer, I was in Washington, DC, submitting paperwork to the Immigration Department. Although none of the boys had yet come over, Dream Farm, LLC, was proceeding fabulously.

I spied him walking down the street with a statuesque brunette. I don't think he recognized me at first, but he hadn't changed a bit.

"John?" He quickened his pace towards me. "John, you look great!"

I patted my midsection, "I've dropped about fifty pounds."

"How did you manage that?"

"Believe it or not, I quit drinking."

"Really. Why?"

"I don't know. It's nothing I planned. I just sort of lost interest in it."

We caught up quickly there on the sidewalk. He introduced his companion, Lynn, as his barrister. I asked why he was in need of an attorney, but as usual he steered the conversation back to me. I told him how well things were going in New York. The entire contamination issue at closing had been a canard. There was no contamination; all the test borings had been clean. Mary and I decided living in Boston and managing the camp would be too difficult, so we sold our house and moved into one of the farms. It was idyllic.

Zor and I stood there a moment longer enjoying each other's company until a taxi finally stopped. Zor held the door for Lynn and then got in. With the window down in back, we continued to talk.

"You know," I said, "you pretty much destroyed my life."

Zor smiled. "Sometimes you have to destroy a life in order to save it."

I shook my head as the cab started to edge into traffic. "Before you go, any suggestions on what I should do now?"

"Continue to change the world in a positive way."

"How do I do that?"

"That's simple." He winked and tapped his nose twice. "Be you."

Made in the USA
San Bernardino, CA
10 February 2013